ARE WE LIVING IN

SATAN'S

LITTLE SEASON?

EXPOSING HIS CUNNING STRATEGIES
TO DECEIVE THE NATIONS

THEO RHISING

Wild Remnant Publishing
Contact at: wildremnantpublishing@gmail.com

© Copyright 2025

ISBN Paperback: 978-1-0688478-7-5

TABLE OF CONTENTS

PREFACE

Like all significant revelations or discoveries of mysteries and hidden truths, I did not arrive at the findings presented in this work on my own. As one of my mentors once said, *"Most of my best thinking has been done by others."*

And so, I owe an immense debt of gratitude to the many courageous individuals who, for years, have toiled, delving deeply into these matters and exposing the deceptions we are currently under. Some of these truth-seekers faced significant backlash; in certain cases, they even recanted their findings, likely due to extreme external pressures or threats from those in power.

One such individual is the creator of the 7-hour YouTube video titled *The Lost History of the Flat Earth,* known by the pseudonym "Ewaranon." Although I was already a flat-earther before viewing it, this video had a profound effect on me, challenging much of what I thought I knew. As someone who has been a conspiracy researcher since 2002, this was no small feat. Although "Ewaranon" later recanted his video, many viewers observed that his recantation felt uncharacteristic, leading some to believe it may have been forced and fabricated by others.

Nevertheless, *The Lost History of the Flat Earth* was the catalyst that prompted my research into Tartaria and the world's fairs of the 19th and early 20th centuries. This, in turn, led me to the work of Noel Hadley and his YouTube channel, *The Unexpected Cosmology.* It was through Hadley's insightful research that I first encountered the idea that Christ's return and the Millennial Kingdom may already have been fulfilled. Eventually, I discovered various Facebook groups dedicated to these topics, including *Tartaria: The Millennial Kingdom of Jesus Christ*. It was through these groups that I encountered the writings of Allan Cornford, who has explored these subjects extensively in his books. Other noteworthy YouTube channels I enjoy watching include: *My Lunch Break*, which explores various old world buildings' origins and architecture, and Paul Stobbs' *Understanding Conspiracy* channel, which goes in depth about the Nephilim of old (who looked like clowns) and little season eschatology.

And so, for me, the pursuit of truth continues—on and on, ever forward.

With this preface, I also wish to express my heartfelt gratitude to all these brave souls who have shared their findings and exposed their innermost thoughts and beliefs for the world to see. These individuals have faced disbelief, ridicule, and derision, often being labeled as "heretics," "fools," and "false teachers." Yet, they persist, undeterred, driven by an unrelenting hunger and passion for truth. To each of you, from the bottom of my heart, I extend my deepest thanks.

And so, dear reader, I hope the information you find in this book will encourage you, challenge you, and spur you to look up these matters more in depth; to embark on, or to further, your own quest for truth. I hope and pray, also, that the Father in heaven accompanies you and blesses you on this brave and often unpredictable journey.

Sincerely,

The Author

INTRODUCTION

I n the annals of interpreting the biblical prophetic timeline, Revelation 20 stands as a profoundly enigmatic chapter. It paints a picture of an epic cosmic conflict and divine sovereignty that stretches beyond the temporal boundaries of our history. The passage presents a dramatic scene: an angel descending from heaven with a key to the bottomless pit and a great chain in hand, tasked with binding the dragon, that ancient serpent who is the Devil, for a thousand years. This binding is a pivotal moment, marking the commencement of Christ's millennial reign—a period of divine rule on earth that promises peace and justice under the sovereign hand of Christ.

The vision of Revelation 20:1-3 is both awe-inspiring and sobering. The angel's descent and the binding of Satan signify a temporary but decisive restriction placed upon the prince of darkness. For a millennium, the dragon is confined in darkness, rendering him incapable of deceiving the nations. This period, often referred to as the "millennial kingdom," represents an era of unprecedented spiritual and moral order, where Christ's reign along with his saints, restores harmony and righteousness.

But, tucked away in this whole Kingdom narrative is a verse that is seldom explored—verse 3. It says, *"And cast him into the bottomless pit, and shut him up, and set a seal upon him, that he should deceive the nations no more, till the thousand years should be fulfilled:* **and after that he must be loosed a little season.***"*

So, as the thousand years come to an end, a startling event unfolds: Satan is released from his prison for what is referred to as a "little season." The exact duration of this season has been widely debated. Some suggest it spans 250 years, while others propose 400. No one really knows. Although opinions differ on its length, many believe we are nearing its climax, with the culmination being a brief assault on "the camp of the saints", followed by swift divine intervention to bring Satan and evil to its final end (see Revelation 20:7-10).

The concept of "Satan's little season" in Revelation 20:3 is one that has been largely overlooked or misunderstood in many Christian teachings. For years, when we were taught about the book of Revelation, the emphasis was often placed on the events of the future—the rise of Antichrist, the Tribulation, and Christ's eventual return. Yet, Revelation 20:3 mentions a period when Satan is "bound" for a thousand years, after which he will be "loosed for a little season." This "little season" has traditionally been taught from a futurist perspective, focusing on a time in the distant future when Satan would have one final reign of terror. However, this interpretation has left many of us unaware of how this period could apply to our present age or what its implications could be on the world today.

The idea of Satan being loosed for "a little season" to "deceive the nations" raises a significant and unsettling question: How would the world look under the full weight of his deceptive ability?

While we often think of Satan's deception as an immediate, overt form of evil—like a sudden, dramatic takeover of governments or societies—it's more likely that it would be a subtle, pervasive influence, deeply integrated into the fabric of human society for decades, even centuries. Given that much of the modern world already struggles with issues of materialism, moral relativism, and spiritual apathy, I would argue that we are already in the thick of this deception. Let's be honest, a world where Satan has fully seduced the nations might not look dramatically different from our current reality.

If Satan were to seduce all nations, would they even know they were in his "little season"? It's a sobering thought that the nations might not even recognize the depth of their current deception. The "little season" could be marked not by obvious chaos or anarchy, but by a false sense of peace and security. People may think they are thriving or evolving, unaware that they are being led astray by a force that has deeply infiltrated all levels of society—culture, politics, education, and even religion. Deception, by its very nature, is most powerful when it's undetected—like a prison without the bars. The inhabitants of the world might be so wrapped in their own beliefs and illusions that they wouldn't even realize they were in the midst of Satan's most subtle and effective work, operating in plain sight. As they say, *"when you're deceived, you have no idea you're being deceived."*

So, the release of Satan from the pit is not merely a return to old patterns of evil, but a calculated resurgence aimed at subverting the divine order established during the millennium. It is during this "little season" that Satan's strategies to corrupt, deceive, and lead astray become most evident, highlighting the intensity and scope of his final assault on humanity.

The subsequent impact of Satan's release from the pit is both profound and far-reaching. In the aftermath of his release, which I believe occurred in or around 1776, we observe a calculated series of maneuvers designed to erase the memory of Christ's reign and establish a new, deceptive order—a "NOVUS ORDO SECLORUM" or New Order of the [Secular] Ages (as stated on the U.S. dollar bill). And, make no mistake, this New World Order is already established. It didn't come about when president George Bush first mentioned it in a speech in 1991. It was already an ongoing process for decades at the time. This lengthy and gradual process involved several key strategies that we will be exploring at length:

- **Historical Revisionism:** The first and most insidious tactic involves rewriting history to obscure the truth of Christ's millennial rule. This historical erasure includes the destruction of physical evidence, such as the abandonment and concealment of cities that once flourished under Christ's reign. The Freemasons, discovering these abandoned cities, meticulously repurpose and conceal their divine origins to support a secular and Luciferian narrative.

- **Mud Floods and Fires:** The mud flood theory posits that a global cataclysm buried advanced civilizations, erasing their history and enabling the creation of a revised narrative by the new architects of history. Some proponents link this event to the release of Satan from the abyss during the "Satan's Little Season," following Christ's thousand-year reign. Evidence cited includes partially buried buildings and photographs of muddied streets in historical images. Additionally, the records of massive fires consuming numerous cities—often described as widespread and suspicious—are believed to have played a role in this reset. These events may have facilitated the rise of new systems of control, with displaced children transported via orphan trains and survivors either manipulated, silenced, or imprisoned.

- **Elite Pacts and Control:** Influential families and elite groups, such as the Rothschilds and Rockefellers, are said to have entered into a pact with Satan upon his release. This agreement grants them substantial power and control over global resources and political systems, consolidating their influence in a world now ripe for manipulation. The pact allows these elites to reshape global structures to align with Luciferian principles, thereby extending their dominion and ensuring that the true nature of the millennial reign remains obscured.

- **Cultural and Educational Manipulation:** The infiltration of educational systems and cultural institutions is employed to perpetuate a secular and materialistic worldview. This manipulation includes the reformation of historical narratives, the promotion of secular ideologies, the corruption of Christianity, and the suppression of spiritual truths. Through propaganda, the masses are conditioned to ignore or reject the divine origins of their world, focusing instead on secular concerns.

- **Technological and Media Influence:** The development and control of technologies such as television, radio, the internet, and now AI, become powerful tools for disseminating Luciferian doctrines. These platforms shape public opinion, manipulate political outcomes, censor information, and create a dominant narrative that marginalizes truth.

- **Globalization and Environmentalism:** The push for globalization and the manipulation of environmental movements serve as mechanisms for implementing a New World Order. By promoting climate change agendas and global regulations, The Ruling Class use these created issues to erode national sovereignties and centralize control under a Luciferian global regime.

- **Surveillance and Control:** The rise of mass surveillance and the police state is another critical aspect of Satan's strategy. The use of technology to monitor and control populations ensures that any dissent against the New World Order is swiftly identified, censored and/or suppressed.
- **False Narratives and Distractions:** Satan's final season is marked by the creation of multiple and regular false flag events and distractions that divert attention from the true spiritual battle. These events are used to justify increased government control, manipulate public fear, reinforce the Luciferian agenda, and most of all, keep populations and individuals in a constant state of fear and trauma—which keeps them more easily under mind control.

In this comprehensive examination, we'll explore how these strategies unfolded in a meticulously orchestrated decades and centuries-long plan to seduce the nations and establish a Luciferian order. The insights presented in this book offer a profound understanding of how the forces of evil have sought to subvert Yahweh's divine order and manipulate human history. By revealing these strategies, we aim to uncover some of the hidden mechanisms at play and illuminate the ongoing spiritual struggle that continues to shape our world.

Get ready to embark on a journey that challenges conventional wisdom and uncovers the layers of deception woven in the aftermath of Satan's release from the abyss—an event that may have occurred around 1776.

According to the American Dollar bill, The NOVUS ORDO SECLORUM (New Order of the [Secular] Ages), began in MDCCLXXVI (1776). It is also the date of the American Declaration of Independence, the date on the book carried by the Statue of Liberty, and the date of the Founding of the Illuminati. Could it also be the date Satan got freed from the pit?

CHAPTER 1

What If I Told You...

"The Matrix is a system, Neo. That system is our enemy. But when you're inside, you look around, what do you see? Businessmen, teachers, lawyers, carpenters. The very minds of the people we are trying to save. But until we do, these people are still a part of that system and that makes them our enemy. You have to understand, most of these people are not ready to be unplugged. And many of them are so inured, so hopelessly dependent on the system, that they will fight to protect it."

~Morpheus, The Matrix (movie)

Do you remember that pivotal scene in *The Matrix* where Morpheus leans in and asks Neo, "What if I told you...?" It's a moment that challenges everything Neo thought he knew, inviting him to consider a reality far different from what he'd ever imagined.

In this chapter, I invite you to your own "Matrix" moment—a challenge to the conventional understanding of biblical prophecy.

What if I told you... that Christ's return and the establishment of His millennial kingdom have already occurred in the first century?

I know. Baloney, right? Perhaps you're even thinking I've lost my marbles? Nevertheless, I urge you to keep reading.

This provocative idea (that Christ might have already returned and ruled for a thousand years) challenges traditional views of eschatology and invites us to reconsider the scriptural evidence surrounding Christ's promises. Many passages in the New Testament suggest that His return was imminent, and some scholars argue that the events described in Revelation—such as the binding of Satan and the reign of Christ—could have been fulfilled within the generation of the early Church. Could it be that we've misunderstood the timing of these profound prophecies? Let's explore the possibility that the millennial reign of Christ has already taken place, and that we are now living in a post-millennial age.

To paraphrase Morpheus: "You take the blue pill—you stop reading here, the story ends, you keep believing whatever you want to believe. You take the red pill—you keep reading and I show you how deep the rabbit hole goes.

The Case for an Imminent Return of Christ in the First Century

1. **Scriptural Basis**: The New Testament includes multiple verses where Christ and the apostles indicate an imminent return of Jesus within the generation that witnessed His ministry. As outlined in verses like Matthew 24:34, Matthew 16:28, and Mark 9:1, Jesus directly tells His disciples that "this generation shall not pass" until all prophesied events, including His return, come to pass. The apostles similarly write about an approaching end, as seen in verses like Romans 13:11 ("for now is our salvation nearer than when we believed") and James 5:8 ("for the coming of the Lord draweth nigh").

2. **Historical Context**: Proponents of this theory argue that the early Christians genuinely believed they were living in the end times, as evidenced by the urgency in the writings of Paul, Peter, and James. The destruction of Jerusalem in A.D. 70 is often seen as a fulfillment of much of these prophecies, marking a significant apocalyptic event for the early church. This historical cataclysm could have been viewed by early Christians as part of Christ's return in judgment upon Israel, giving further weight to the argument that they expected His return within their lifetime.

3. **Consistent with Early Church Expectations**: The earliest Christians were anticipating an imminent return, and their writings reflect this. By interpreting Christ's return as happening soon after His resurrection, this theory remains faithful to the expectations of those early believers, who were instructed to be watchful and prepared for Christ's return during their own lifetimes.

To Seal or Not to Seal, That Is the Question

The Book of Daniel and the Book of Revelation are two of the Bible's most compelling prophetic texts, offering profound insights into God's plan for humanity. Yet, these books present a striking contrast in how their messages were to be handled. Daniel, who lived around 600 BC, in a time when the fulfillment of his visions lay far in the future, was commanded:

"Seal the book, even to the time of the end: many shall run to and fro, and knowledge shall be increased." ~Daniel 12:4

Meanwhile, John, writing the Book of Revelation centuries later, was told:

"Seal not the sayings of the prophecy of this book: for the time is at hand." ~Revelation 22:10

Why was Daniel's prophecy sealed for a distant time, while Revelation's was declared urgent and immediate? This stark difference raises profound questions about the nature of these prophecies, the flow of history, and the timing of God's divine plan. Could the unsealing of Revelation signal that its fulfillment was imminent for John's audience?

What do these instructions reveal about the unfolding of prophetic events? Are we living in the later era foretold by the unsealed prophecies of Revelation? The answers may challenge everything you thought you knew about biblical eschatology.

Jesus Said the Kingdom of God Was Coming "Soon"

Jesus' mission was to seek and save the lost, preaching repentance and declaring that the "kingdom of God" was near— at hand. Throughout His ministry, He warned of a quickly approaching time when people needed to repent and believe His message to avoid the consequences that would follow. The coming of the kingdom was not a distant event but one that He emphasized as imminent.

God the Father gave Jesus the revelation of Himself to show His followers "what must shortly come to pass" (Revelation 1:1). Jesus spoke repeatedly of the kingdom of God being "at hand"— implying that the fulfillment of God's plans was immediate, not thousands of years in the future. He used terms like "at hand," meaning imminent, and phrases like "I come quickly," to stress the urgency of His return. Jesus intended for His words to be understood as happening soon, and the Apostles likewise conveyed this urgency to their own generation, believing the events He spoke of were at hand in their day.

Mark 1:14-15 records this urgency in Jesus' message: *"Now after that John was put in prison, Jesus came into Galilee, preaching the gospel of the kingdom of God, and saying,* The time is fulfilled, and the kingdom of God is at hand: repent ye, and believe the gospel." Similarly, Matthew 4:17 captures Jesus' call for repentance because *"the kingdom of heaven is at hand."* The Apostles took these statements to heart, understanding that they were to prepare for events they believed would occur in their own lifetimes.

In Revelation 22:6, 10, and 12, we read: "And he said unto me, *These sayings are faithful and true: and the Lord God of the holy prophets sent his angel to shew unto his servants the things which must shortly be done... Seal not the sayings of the prophecy of this book: for the time is at hand... Behold, I come quickly."* These words reiterate that the timing of Jesus' return was imminent.

Some Standing Here Will Not Taste Death

In biblical hermeneutics, the principle of contextualization is critical for accurately interpreting the meaning of the Scriptures. Contextualization involves considering the historical, cultural, and linguistic context of a text to understand its original intent and application. A primary question in biblical interpretation is: Who was the text originally written for, and who was Jesus addressing when He spoke those words? This understanding shapes the way we interpret His messages, as they were not spoken to people living 2,000 years later, but to those standing in front of Him in His time.

In the case of Matthew 16:27-28, where Jesus states, "There be some standing here, which shall not taste of death, till they see the Son of man coming in his kingdom," it is crucial to recognize that His words were directed to His immediate audience, the disciples and followers who were with Him in that moment. While it is often tempting for later readers, especially those in modern times, to interpret these statements in the context of an event yet to come, this passage, like many others, was meant to be understood in the context of the people who first heard it.

Jesus was not speaking to distant future generations, but to the people who were listening to Him on that very day. He made it clear that some of those standing with Him would see the fulfillment of His promise within their lifetime. This points to the imminent nature of His kingdom coming in glory, which many of His followers at the time understood as something that would occur shortly after His teachings, possibly linked to His death, resurrection, and the events surrounding the destruction of the temple in Jerusalem in 70 A.D.

The misunderstanding of this passage, often referred to in futurist interpretations, arises when we fail to consider the context of Jesus' audience. He was addressing the people in front of Him, and they took His words to mean that they would witness His return in their lifetime. Therefore, understanding the historical and situational context of the texts is essential. In the case of Matthew 16:27-28, the coming of the Son of Man in glory was not a distant event for a future generation but a promise to the people of that time that they would witness something transformative within their lifetimes. The concept of the "kingdom of God" was not purely spiritual, as many might interpret it today, but was closely tied to the historical and cultural realities of the people of first-century Judea.

By focusing on who Jesus was speaking to and why these words were relevant to them, we can more accurately grasp the message that Jesus was conveying. This does not negate the broader, ongoing significance of Christ's kingdom, but it does remind us that the original hearers were integral to understanding the text. In biblical hermeneutics, failure to recognize the context of Jesus' immediate audience often leads to misinterpretation or anachronistic reading, distorting the meaning of His words for those He originally intended to hear them.

The Apostles Believed the Kingdom Was Coming Soon

The Apostles believed that the kingdom of God was indeed near. In 1 Peter 4:7, Peter writes, *"But the end of all things is at hand: be ye therefore sober, and watch unto prayer."* Similarly, in James 5:7, James encourages believers to remain patient, saying, *"Be patient therefore, brethren, unto the coming of the Lord..."* The use of language like "at hand" and "soon" reflects the Apostles' belief that Jesus' return was imminent in their generation.

Paul also speaks in terms that imply immediacy. In Romans 13:11-12, he writes, "And that, knowing the time, that now it is high time to awake out of sleep: for now is our salvation nearer than when we believed. *The night is far spent, the day is at hand."* Paul's sense of urgency in this message shows that he, too, believed the return of Jesus was soon.

But Lord, What About Him (John)?

When Jesus told the Apostles that some of them might live to see His return, it led to speculation that the Apostle John would remain alive until that day. In John 21:22-23, Jesus said to Peter, *"If I will that he [John] tarry till I come, what is that to thee? Follow thou me."* This statement fueled hope among early Christians that the apostle John might witness Jesus' return within his lifetime, reinforcing the belief that Jesus' second coming would happen within their generation.

Angels Indicated to His Apostles That Jesus Would Come Back Soon

The angels who appeared to Jesus' many followers at His ascension also affirmed this sense of imminence. Acts 1:10-11 records, "And while they looked steadfastly toward heaven as he went up, behold, two men stood by them in white apparel; which also said, *Ye men of Galilee, why stand ye gazing up into heaven? This same Jesus... shall so come in like manner as ye have seen him go into heaven.*" This promise was given directly to a crowd of 500, who expected to see the fulfillment of Jesus' return soon.

This instance, combined with the clear emphasis on "soon" and "at hand" throughout Jesus' teachings, and the Apostles' writings, strongly suggests that they expected His return within their own generation.

N.T. Verses Indicating Christ's Expected Soon Return

Here's a list of verses from the King James Version (KJV) of the Bible where Christ or the apostles hint at a close return of Christ, possibly within the generation of the first-century audience He was addressing. I've organized them chronologically based on their placement in the New Testament.

Gospels:

1. **Matthew 10:23**

   "But when they persecute you in this city, flee ye into another: for verily I say unto you, Ye shall not have gone over the cities of Israel, till the Son of man be come."

- o Jesus suggests that His return will occur before the cities of Israel have all been reached by His fleeing followers.

2. **Matthew 16:28**

"Verily I say unto you, There be some standing here, which shall not taste of death, till they see the Son of man coming in his kingdom."

- o Jesus indicates that some of those present would witness His return before they die.

3. **Matthew 24:34**

"Verily I say unto you, This generation shall not pass, till all these things be fulfilled."

- o Jesus speaks about the events leading up to His return, asserting that they will happen within the current generation.

4. **Mark 9:1**

"And he said unto them, Verily I say unto you, That there be some of them that stand here, which shall not taste of death, till they have seen the kingdom of God come with power."

- o Similar to Matthew 16:28, Jesus implies that some people will see the kingdom of God before they die.

5. **Mark 13:30**

"Verily I say unto you, that this generation shall not pass, till all these things be done."

- o Echoing Matthew 24:34, Jesus affirms that the events described will occur within that generation.

6. **Luke 9:27**

"But I tell you of a truth, there be some standing here, which shall not taste of death, till they see the kingdom of God."

- o This verse parallels Mark 9:1, suggesting that some will witness the kingdom of God before their death.

7. **Luke 21:32**

"Verily I say unto you, This generation shall not pass away, till all be fulfilled."

- o Similar to Matthew 24:34 and Mark 13:30, Jesus states that the generation of His time will see the fulfillment of these prophetic events.

8. **John 14:2-3**

"In my Father's house are many mansions... I will come again and receive you to Myself; that where I am, there you may be also."

- o Jesus promises a near return to his followers.

9. **John 14:18-19**

"I will not leave you as orphans; I will come to you... the world will no longer see Me, but you will see Me."

- o He reassures his disciples of a soon return.

10. **John 16:16-17**

"A little while, and you will no longer see Me; and again a little while, and you will see Me."

- o The phrase suggests a quick return they would witness.

11. **John 21:22-23**

   "If I want him to remain until I come, what is that to you?"

   - o This statement led early Christians to believe in a potential imminent return.

Epistles:

1. **Romans 13:11**

   "And that, knowing the time, that now it is high time to awake out of sleep: for now is our salvation nearer than when we believed."

   - o Paul suggests that the coming of salvation is near, indicating an imminent return.

2. **1 Corinthians 7:29**

   "But this I say, brethren, the time is short: it remaineth, that both they that have wives be as though they had none."

   - o Paul emphasizes the shortness of the time, implying a close return of Christ.

3. **1 Corinthians 10:11**

   "Now all these things happened unto them for ensamples: and they are written for our admonition, upon whom the ends of the world are come."

   - o Paul refers to the end of the world as imminent for his audience.

4. **Philippians 4:5**

   "Let your moderation be known unto all men. The Lord is at hand."

   - o Paul hints that the Lord's return is near.

5. **1 Thessalonians 4:15**

"For this we say unto you by the word of the Lord, that we which are alive and remain unto the coming of the Lord shall not prevent them which are asleep."

   o Paul indicates that some of his audience might still be alive at the coming of the Lord.

6. **1 Thessalonians 5:2**

"For yourselves know perfectly that the day of the Lord so cometh as a thief in the night."

   o Paul describes the day of the Lord as coming unexpectedly, reinforcing the idea of its imminence.

7. **2 Thessalonians 2:2**

"That ye be not soon shaken in mind, or be troubled, neither by spirit, nor by word, nor by letter as from us, as that the day of Christ is at hand."

   o Paul reassures the Thessalonians that the day of Christ is approaching, countering claims that it has already occurred.

8. **Hebrews 10:37**

"For yet a little while, and he that shall come will come, and will not tarry."

   o The author of Hebrews speaks of the coming of Christ as imminent.

9. **James 5:8**

"Be ye also patient; stablish your hearts: for the coming of the Lord draweth nigh."

   o James encourages patience, noting that the Lord's return is near.

10. **Revelation 1:3**

"Blessed is he that readeth, and they that hear the words of this prophecy, and keep those things which are written therein: for the time is at hand."

- o John indicates that the time for the fulfillment of these prophecies is near.

11. **Revelation 3:11**

"Behold, I come quickly: hold that fast which thou hast, that no man take thy crown."

- o Jesus promises a swift return, urging perseverance.

12. **Revelation 22:7**

"Behold, I come quickly: blessed is he that keepeth the sayings of the prophecy of this book."

- o Jesus again emphasizes His imminent return.

13. **Revelation 22:12**

"And, behold, I come quickly; and my reward is with me, to give every man according as his work shall be."

- o Jesus reaffirms that His return is near and that He will bring rewards.

14. **Revelation 22:20**

"He which testifieth these things saith, Surely I come quickly. Amen. Even so, come, Lord Jesus."

- o John concludes the book with a declaration of Jesus's imminent return.

After reading these verses from *a new angle* and *in a new light*, isn't it preposterous to say that Christ and the apostles were all wrong about the timing of His return? These scriptural assurances reflect a genuine expectation that was foundational to their faith and ministry.

Did He Indeed Return Around 70AD?

The lack of extensive documentation about Christ's return and the Millennium is striking and raises questions about why these monumental events seem shrouded in mystery. This absence can be attributed to the systematic concealment, destruction, or suppression of books, texts, and other historical proofs. Whether through deliberate burning of libraries, alteration of manuscripts, or the erasure of inconvenient truths, evidence of these events has been effectively obscured. Those in power during Satan's Little Season likely sought to rewrite history, ensuring that humanity would remain ignorant of Christ's reign and His victorious return around 70-73 AD. I suspect many of these proof texts can be found in the underground libraries of the Vatican.

Nevertheless, the possibility that Christ returned around 70-73 AD has its roots in both scriptural prophecy and historical accounts from that time, pointing to an event of immense spiritual and eschatological significance. In the Gospel of Matthew (chapter 24), Jesus prophesies signs that would precede "the end of the age" and His coming, including wars, earthquakes, and celestial signs. He emphasizes that these things would happen within "this generation," leading many to conclude that His words were meant for those alive in the first century.

Historian Tacitus provides a chilling account of supernatural events that seem to align with these prophecies, writing that *"In the sky appeared a vision of armies in conflict, of glittering armour. A sudden lightning flash from the clouds lit up the*

Temple. The doors of the holy place abruptly opened, a superhuman voice was heard to declare that God was leaving it, and in the same instant came the rushing tumult of departure" (*Histories*, Book 5, v. 13). Such extraordinary events—seen as omens or supernatural interventions—suggest that God's presence was visibly and audibly withdrawing from Jerusalem just before the city's destruction.

Josephus, another historian of the period, corroborates this with his own startling account: *"Before sun-setting, chariots and troops of soldiers in their armor were seen running about in the clouds, and surrounding cities... they heard a sound as of a great multitude, saying 'Let us remove hence'"* (*Jewish Wars*, VI-V-3). Such visions and sounds reported by multiple eyewitnesses point to celestial events that would naturally be seen as divine signs of judgment and the conclusion of an era. These occurrences align with the prophetic language of Christ's return as described in the Gospels, as though the heavens themselves were bearing witness to a monumental spiritual shift.

Finally, Eusebius, the early Christian historian, records similar phenomena: *"For before the setting of the sun chariots and armed troops were seen throughout the whole region in mid-air, wheeling through the clouds and encircling the cities"* (*Ecclesiastical History*, Book 3, Chapter 8).

Taken together, these accounts suggest that the heavens displayed striking signs, which many interpreted as indicators of divine intervention.

With all of these firsthand testimonies—Tacitus, Josephus, and Eusebius—supporting the occurrence of supernatural events, some argue that Christ's return may have already happened. This view posits that the fall of Jerusalem and the destruction of the Temple signaled the end of the old covenant and the beginning of the new, fulfilling Christ's prophecy within the timeline He set for His followers.

The Destruction of Jerusalem in 70-73 AD,
Engraving by Louis Haghe (1806-85)

CHAPTER 2:

Debunking Futurism

"Jesus thought that the history of the world would come to a screeching halt, that God would intervene in the affairs of this planet, overthrow the forces of evil in a cosmic act of judgment, and establish his utopian kingdom here on earth. And this was to happen within Jesus' own generation." ~Bart D. Ehrman, New Testament scholar emeritus, author of *Jesus: Apocalyptic Prophet of the New Millenium*

In this chapter, we will delve into the popular eschatological view known as *futurism* and examine its claims in light of Scripture and historical context. Futurism, which holds that many prophetic events—such as the rise of the Antichrist, the Mark of the Beast, the Great Tribulation, and the Second Coming of Christ—are yet to occur, has shaped much of modern (and Western) Christian thought. For the record, I adhered to the eschatological position of futurism from the moment I became a Christian, and I maintained that belief for over 35 years. In my late teens and early twenties, I read books by Hal Lindsey, Jack Van Impe, and Paul Lalonde, to name just a few.

However, a few years ago, when presented with this new information and after studying it for myself, I realized that the interpretation I had always held might not have been as accurate as I had been led to believe by the authorities in churches and seminaries. A closer examination of the Bible and the early Church's understanding of prophecy revealed that the commonly accepted interpretation may not be as reliable as we've been led to think. Or, could it be that all of it was contrived and aimed at deceiving us?

Futurism's Popularity and Promotion

1. **Futurism's Rise in the 19th Century**: The futurist interpretation of prophecy gained significant traction during the 19th century, primarily through the works of scholars like John Nelson Darby, who introduced the idea of a "rapture" and placed much of Revelation's events in the distant future. This view, which sees the Second Coming, tribulation, and millennial reign as events that have not yet occurred, quickly became the dominant eschatological framework in many Christian denominations, particularly among Evangelicals and Dispensationalists.

2. **The Influence of John Nelson Darby (1800–1882):** A Bible teacher and leader of the Plymouth Brethren, is widely regarded as the father of modern futurism and dispensationalism. His theological perspective, emphasizing the doctrine of imminency, gave rise to futurism, which focuses on prophetic events like the rapture and the seven-year Tribulation. Darby's translations of the Bible further solidified his influence on these doctrines. As the originator of premillennial, pretribulational dispensationalism, Darby advanced a literal interpretation of Scripture, highlighting a distinct

separation between the church and national Israel. He shaped a movement that placed strong emphasis on biblical prophecy and the Second Coming of Christ.

3. **The Influence of C.I. Scofield (1843-1921)**: Another pivotal figure in popularizing futurism was C.I. Scofield, whose *Scofield Reference Bible* became one of the most influential tools for promoting dispensational theology. Scofield built upon Darby's ideas, embedding them in detailed study notes that linked biblical passages to a dispensational timeline, emphasizing future events like the rapture and the tribulation. His work, which gained significant traction in evangelical circles, also drew scrutiny due to his possible connections with Freemasonry. Some researchers suggest that Scofield's promotion of futurism aligns with broader agendas that may have sought to shape Christian eschatology for political and spiritual purposes.

4. **Widely Promoted and Institutionalized:** The futurist model has been heavily promoted in modern church teaching, popular literature, and especially through the publication of prophetic books like Hal Lindsey's The Late Great Planet Earth and the Left Behind series by Tim LaHaye and Jerry B. Jenkins. These books, along with many others and popular media, have profoundly influenced modern Christian thought, embedding the futurist narrative deeply into popular culture.

5. **Hollywood's Role**: Hollywood has also played a significant role in perpetuating the futurist interpretation of prophecy. Films like *Left Behind, The Omega Code,* and apocalyptic-themed movies like *The Day After Tomorrow* or *Armageddon* subtly reinforce

futurist ideas by depicting global catastrophe as a future event and making it seem like a dramatic, impending occurrence. This saturation in popular culture serves to normalize the belief that the end times are an approaching event, rather than something that has already occurred—biblically speaking.

6. **A Cunning Deception?**: It could be argues that this overwhelming promotion of futurism could be part of a larger spiritual deception. If Satan has been released, and the Millenium already happened, one strategy could be to lull Christians into a state of spiritual-opium-induced complacency. By promoting a futurist view, Christians are distracted from realizing that significant biblical events have already transpired and that Satan is currently active in deceiving the nations. This aligns with the notion that Satan, once released from the pit, would "deceive the nations" (Revelation 20:7-8) and lead them astray through severe misinformation and altered historical narratives.

7. **Futurism as a Tool for Control**: Futurism also serves as a tool for controlling Christian eschatology, keeping believers focused on external future events rather than the present reality and level of spiritual warfare. The widespread promotion of this interpretation by influential figures, institutions, and media can be seen as a means to shift attention away from the historical and spiritual significance of the past millennium, thereby blinding people to Satan's current work in the world. It's the best and brightest of his deceptions.

8. **Faking the Apocalypse:** In a world where the ruling elites exert significant influence over global events, it's possible that some of the catastrophic occurrences we

witness today—pandemics, political upheavals, natural disasters—are not merely the result of chance or misfortune, but are being engineered to mimic and resemble the apocalyptic events described in the Book of Revelation. By doing so, these elites could be attempting to keep the Christian population blind and complacent, locked into a futuristic mindset, and unaware that we are already living in Satan's "little season."

The promotion of these manufactured crises could serve a dual purpose: to divert attention away from the fact that the true biblical events have already occurred, and to deepen the spiritual deception by creating an illusion of fulfillment. As the masses focus on what they believe are the signs of the end times, they remain unaware that the ultimate deception has already taken place. The historical and spiritual implications of Satan's release are obscured, and the Church continues to wait for a return that may never come (not the way they think), thus playing into the hands of those who seek to control both the narrative and the minds of the masses.

Through these artificially constructed crises, the ruling powers are ensuring that Christians remain in a state of false expectation—waiting for the rapture and the apocalypse, while blind to where they are in its timeline.

Comparing the Two Theories

Believing that Christ has already returned, established His Millennial Kingdom, and that Satan was indeed bound and cast into the abyss for 1,000 years can profoundly transform how you experience and perceive life as a believer.

Back when I was a futurist, my wife and I endured numerous trials and difficulties within just a few years—much of which we attributed to spiritual warfare—which it was. We would fast, pray, and repeat the cycle, yet the results often felt discouragingly minimal. I vividly remember her saying to me, *"If we truly have victory over all the power of the enemy, why is it so hard? Why don't we see it?"* At the time, I had few answers and began to question the Bible itself, not realizing that we were living in a period when Satan had been released and wielded far more influence and power than before. This misunderstanding serves as just one example of the struggles believers face when they fail to discern the times and seasons we are in. Here are some of the other far-reaching implications of gaining clarity on these crucial matters.

- **Historical Fulfillment**: The little season theory places significant prophetic fulfillment in the first century, with the millennial reign beginning not long after 70 AD—physically on the Earth. In contrast, futurism projects the fulfillment of most of these prophecies (Daniel, Revelation, Matthew 24) into the future, awaiting the tribulation, rapture, and a literal thousand-year reign.

- **Impact on Christian Living**: Those who hold to the little season theory might argue that it leads to greater urgency in recognizing Satan's powerful influence in the world and striving for more vigilance, awareness, and faithfulness. On the other hand, futurists emphasize preparation for a future rapture, often believed to happen before the tribulation, thus sparing them from wrath and harm. This could have the unintended consequence of making futurist believers complacent in the face of present challenges; not to mention completely oblivious to the reality of biblical times and seasons.

- **Faith in Jesus' Integrity**: The realization that Jesus' prophecy about His return—specifically that it would occur within "this generation" (Matthew 24:34; Mark 13:30; Luke 21:32)—was true can be deeply faith-affirming for believers. It showcases His unwavering trustworthiness, truthfulness, and divine authority. Jesus' words, *"Heaven and earth will pass away, but my words will never pass away"* (Matthew 24:35), reassure us that His promises are reliable. Far from undermining faith, understanding that His return was fulfilled as He said, emphasizes His role as the ultimate truth-bearer and the fulfillment of prophecy, reinforcing confidence in *all His teachings.*

- **Encouragement for Believers**: For those who accept this interpretation, it can transform their view of Scripture from one of waiting to one of assurance. Instead of questioning whether Jesus' and the apostle's words were misunderstood or delayed, believers can find comfort in the firm knowledge and assurance that God's plan unfolded precisely as foretold—and quickly! This perspective builds trust in Yahweh, and in the Bible's consistency and the reliability.

- **Strengthening Faith and Purpose**: Recognizing that Jesus kept His word about His return encourages a re-evaluation of what it means to live as His follower today. Believers are called to live in light of His accomplished victory, knowing they are already part of His kingdom (Luke 17:20-21). This can inspire a deeper commitment to faith, a greater reliance on Scripture, and a better focus on fulfilling the mission of spreading truth, the Gospel, and advancing His kingdom. Besides, we know what we're waiting for now, a New Heaven and a New Earth. This, too, has a non negligible impact.

The theory of a first-century return of Christ and Satan's current season of deception offers an alternative and much needed understanding of biblical prophecy. While futurism unfortunately remains the dominant narrative, deceptively reinforced by Christian institutions, media, and even Hollywood; the case can be made that it may serve as part of a broader deception—one that ultimately deceives believers.

Okay, So, If Not in the Future, Then What About...

If futurism is not the correct lens through which to interpret Revelation and other eschatological passages, it leaves many wondering and rightfully asking: How should we understand the Antichrist, the False Prophet, the Mark of the Beast, the "Rapture", the Tribulation, and other apocalyptic themes? The "little season" view does provide a coherent, historical understanding of these elements, grounded in Scripture and historical events.

So, let's explore each of these other topics and examine how they align with the historical fulfillment described by the "little season" perspective.

Who Was the Antichrist?

The beast in Revelation was prophesied to have authority "to make war on the saints and to conquer them" for a period of 42 months, with power over "every tribe and people and language and nation" (Revelation 13:5-7). Historically, Nero's persecution of Christians aligns precisely with this timeframe. Beginning in November 64 AD and ending with his suicide in June 68 AD, his campaign against Christians lasted exactly 42 months.

The saints were encouraged to endure and remain faithful, as the beast who lived by the sword would ultimately die by it (Revelation 13:10, 14). Nero's death by suicide occurred when he thrust his own sword into his throat, assisted by his secretary, Epaphroditus. This act followed his waning popularity and an attempted coup. Early Christian writers, like Tertullian (145-220 AD), credited "Nero's cruel sword" with providing the martyr's blood that became the seed of the church. Tertullian noted Nero as the first Roman emperor to wage imperial persecution against Christians.

Revelation describes the beast from the sea as receiving support from a second beast "from the earth," compelling "the earth and its inhabitants" to worship the first beast. Statues of Nero were erected, and accounts from writers such as Dio Cassius describe events where foreign kings, like Tiridates, worshipped Nero and his images. Statues of Nero were reportedly made to appear alive, and those who refused to worship these images faced execution (Revelation 13:11-15).

The mark of the beast, placed on the right hand or forehead, represented allegiance to Nero and Rome. Historical evidence shows that individuals in the Roman Empire were required to burn incense and declare, "Caesar is Lord." Compliance granted them a certificate or *libellus*, which allowed participation in commerce. Without it, they could neither buy nor sell (Revelation 13:16-17).

John's readers were instructed to calculate the beast's number, 666, which pointed directly to Nero. Using Hebrew gematria, Nero's name, "Neron Kaisar" (NRWN QSR), adds up to 666. Some manuscripts reference 616, derived from a Latinized spelling of Nero's name. John likely encoded this information in Hebrew to avoid Roman detection, as he was exiled to Patmos under Roman rule (Revelation 13:18).

The beast is depicted as having ten horns, symbolizing power and authority granted to it by others. Rome, consisting of ten senatorial provinces, used its governors to enforce Nero's persecution of Christians and its war against Jerusalem, culminating in the city's destruction and burning in 70-73 AD (Revelation 13:1; 17:3, 7, 12-17).

The beast's seven heads are identified as the seven hills of Rome and seven kings. Five of these kings had fallen, one reigned during John's time, and another was to come briefly. The first five emperors—Julius Caesar, Augustus, Tiberius, Caligula, and Claudius—preceded Nero, the sixth. The seventh, Galba, reigned briefly before being assassinated (Revelation 17:9-10).

Nero is also connected to the lion imagery in Revelation. The apostle Paul, referring to his trial before Nero, stated he was "rescued from the lion's mouth" (2 Timothy 4:16-17).

One of the beast's heads was said to suffer a mortal wound but recover, causing the world to marvel (Revelation 13:3). Nero's suicide in 68 AD marked the end of the Julio-Claudian dynasty and triggered chaos across the empire. Josephus described the Roman world as "unsettled and tottering" during this period. After Nero, three emperors—Galba, Otho, and Vitellius—reigned briefly, each attempting to revive Nero's image and authority. Stability was restored only when Vespasian took power in 69 AD, and Rome emerged stronger than before.

Nero's reign demanded worship to an extreme degree. He was deified during his lifetime and posthumously. Statues of Nero towered over 110 feet high, and coins celebrated him as "Almighty God" and "Savior." Foreign rulers were compelled to worship him and his images publicly, fulfilling the prophecy that "the whole earth" (interpreted as the Roman Empire or Israel) would marvel and worship the beast (Revelation 13:4, 8; 17:8).

What About the False Prophet?

Just like that of the Antichrist, the identity of the False Prophet described in Revelation 13:11–18, is closely tied to the events surrounding the destruction of Jerusalem in 70-73 AD and the Roman emperors of that time. Revelation 17:10-11 provides a framework for interpreting the succession of Roman rulers, describing seven kings: five fallen (Julius Caesar, Augustus, Tiberius, Caligula, and Claudius), one reigning (Nero during John's writing), and one to come briefly (Vespasian). The Beast, referred to as "the eighth," is said to be "of the seven," aligning with Titus, Vespasian's son and successor. Titus's role in the military conquest of Jerusalem and the destruction of the Temple fits the description of the False Prophet who led people into idolatry and blasphemy.

Titus's actions, such as his leadership during the siege of Jerusalem, the promotion of Roman emperor worship, and the deification of the Flavian dynasty, fulfill key characteristics of the False Prophet. Roman propaganda elevated military victories like those of Titus as divine acts, and favorable omens during his campaigns were framed as miraculous signs. These align with the biblical depiction of the False Prophet deceiving people through wonders and compelling worship of the Beast. While figures like Vespasian or Florus are also considered, Titus's role as the "eighth king" and his involvement in pivotal historical events make him a compelling candidate within this eschatological framework.

Alternative interpretations, however, suggest the False Prophet could represent religious or spiritual leaders of the era, such as Simon Magus, the Pharisees, or Caiaphas, who opposed Christ and misled the people through deception. Others point to figures like Bar Kokhba, whose false hopes led to rebellion. These perspectives expand the role of the False Prophet beyond political figures to include broader forces of spiritual manipulation and distortion of truth, further illustrating the complex and multifaceted nature of this prophetic figure.

What about The Rapture?

Many proponents of the Little Season theory place little to no emphasis on the rapture event. In fact, most I know either outright reject the idea or view it as part of a doctrinal deception. Still, I'll attempt to address the question here.

The resurrection of the saints mentioned in Matthew 27:52-53 is distinct from what is commonly referred to as "the rapture" (a term that does not appear in the Bible). The resurrection described in Matthew occurred during Christ's crucifixion, showcasing His victory over sin and death. By contrast, the rapture is typically associated with Christ's second coming. The apostle Paul addressed confusion about these events in 2 Timothy 2:17-18, particularly regarding the first resurrection. He wrote:

"But shun profane and vain babblings: for they will increase unto more ungodliness. And their word will eat as doth a canker: of whom is Hymenaeus and Philetus; who concerning the truth have erred, saying that the resurrection is past already; and overthrow the faith of some."

Paul's frustration stemmed from false teachings that conflated or misrepresented these events. For example, Matthew 27 records:

"And the graves were opened; and many bodies of the saints which slept arose, and came out of the graves after his resurrection, and went into the holy city, and appeared unto many." ~Matthew 27:52-53

While this was indeed a resurrection, Paul clarified that it was not *the* first resurrection nor was it tied to the rapture.

So, when did the rapture occur? Do we have any records of it? If it happened, it likely looked very different from the Hollywood dramatizations or the depictions in the *Left Behind* series. It may have been limited to the 144,000 saints mentioned in Revelation. Historical accounts provide some intriguing possibilities.

The pagan Roman historian Tacitus (c. A.D. 56-120) recorded this strange event in his Histories:

"Prodigies had occurred, but their expiation by the offering of victims or solemn vows is held to be unlawful by a nation which is the slave of superstition and the enemy of true beliefs. In the sky appeared a vision of armies in conflict, of glittering armor. A sudden lightning flash from the clouds lit up the Temple. The doors of the holy place abruptly opened, a superhuman voice was heard to declare that the gods were leaving it, and in the same instant came the rushing tumult of their departure. Few people placed a sinister interpretation upon this. The majority were convinced that the ancient scriptures of their priests alluded to the present as the very time when the Orient would triumph and from Judaea would go forth men destined to rule the world." (Histories, Book 5, v. 13)

Eusebius of Caesarea (A.D. 263-339), also, says in his Ecclesiastical History:

"For before the setting of the sun chariots and armed troops were seen throughout the whole region in mid-air, wheeling through the clouds and encircling the cities." (Book 3, Ch. 8)

Could the rapture have coincided with these events, linked to the Parousia (the appearing of the Lord Jesus as a conquering King in the heavens)? Alternatively, some suggest the rapture might have occurred at the close of the Millennial Kingdom. This theory posits that cities were left unoccupied as the rapture led into the final resurrection, aligning with Satan's release for his "little season" (Revelation 20:3, 7). In short, I do not have a definitive answer pertaining to the rapture as the question falls in three distinct categories:

1. Maybe it's a false teaching/interpretation and never happened.
2. Maybe it happened, but we have little or no records of it.
3. Maybe it happened, but in a very different context and timing (post-millennial).

What About Babylon the Great/The Great Prostitute?

Babylon is depicted as the Great Prostitute, symbolizing spiritual infidelity and corruption. This label is often associated with Jerusalem, the city that rejected and crucified Christ and persecuted His followers. Its destruction in 70-73 AD marked the judgment of the old covenant system. However, there is also a compelling case for identifying Babylon as Rome, the imperial power that dominated the ancient world and persecuted Christians. The Apostle Peter wrote from "Babylon" while residing in Rome (1 Peter 5:13), underscoring the dual application of this term.

What About the Kingdom of God?

The Kingdom of God, which Jesus extensively preached about, is not just a spiritual experience, as the majority of futurist Christians believe today. It is both a physical and spiritual reality. Spiritually, it refers to heaven, the abode of God, and the everlasting covenant that grants eternal life to believers, initiated through Christ's death, resurrection, and ascension (Luke 17:21). Physically, however, it points to the millennial reign of Christ, where He was to rule with a rod of iron (Revelation 2:27). During this thousand-year period, Christ was to establish His authority as King, fulfilling His promises of restoration and justice, with His saints ruling alongside Him (Luke 19:17).

Life In the Millenium

From the eschatological perspective of the "little season," the Millennium represents a distinct and extraordinary era in human history—one characterized by Christ's physical reign over the earth, aided by His saints. It is a time of unparalleled justice, prosperity, and peace, yet not without sin, conflict, or disobedience among those who did not partake in the first resurrection. This period, as described in Scripture, is distinct from the new heavens and new earth (Revelation 21), where all sin and demonic influences are forever eradicated. The Millennial reign on earth is also distinct from life in heaven—where no corruption is found. Let us then explore what life could have been like during this remarkable age.

Christ's Reign and the Rule of the Saints

Revelation 20:4-6 describes the reign of Christ and His saints during the Millennium. Those who were part of the first resurrection—numbered at 144,000; 12,000 from each tribe of

Israel (Revelation 7:4)—were given authority to reign with Christ. These ascended saints, transformed into glorified bodies, served as priests and kings, fulfilling Revelation 5:10: *"Through your blood, you have made us into priests and kings, and we shall reign on the earth."*

This government of righteousness extended to the cities, city-states, and nations of the world. Christ Himself ruled with a rod of iron (Revelation 2:27), ensuring justice and peace. The saints, empowered with resurrected bodies, wisdom and divine insight, governed regions and cities, fulfilling Christ's promise in Luke 19:17:

"Well done, good servant! Because you have been faithful in a very little, you shall have authority over ten cities."

Their leadership ushered in an era of stability, prosperity, and tremendous innovation.

The Reality of Sin and Disobedience

While the saints were glorified and ruled alongside Christ, the Millennium was not free from sin. Those who survived the judgment of Christ's second coming but were not part of the first resurrection remained mortal, subject to temptation and disobedience. Zechariah 14 provides insight into this dynamic:

"Then the survivors from all the nations that have attacked Jerusalem will go up year after year to worship the King, the Lord Almighty, and to celebrate the Festival of Tabernacles. If any of the peoples of the earth do not go up to Jerusalem to worship the King, the Lord Almighty, they will have no rain." (Zechariah 14:16-17)

This passage reveals that while Christ's rule brought a higher level of peace and justice, participation in His Kingdom's blessings required faithful obedience. Nations or individuals who refused to worship the King every year faced tangible consequences, such as drought and lack of prosperity. The Millennium thus served as a period of probation for the remaining mortals, demonstrating the consequences of disobedience even under ideal conditions.

Old Testament Insights into the Millennium

Several Old Testament prophecies provide vivid descriptions of life during the Millennium. While some passages also anticipate the eternal state of the new heavens and new earth, certain texts specifically refer to the millennial reign:

Isaiah 2:2-4:

"In the last days the mountain of the Lord's temple will be established as the highest of the mountains; it will be exalted above the hills, and all nations will stream to it. Many peoples will come and say, 'Come, let us go up to the mountain of the Lord, to the temple of the God of Jacob. He will teach us his ways, so that we may walk in his paths.' The law will go out from Zion, the word of the Lord from Jerusalem. He will judge between the nations and will settle disputes for many peoples. They will beat their swords into plowshares and their spears into pruning hooks."

Isaiah 65:20:

"Never again will there be in it an infant who lives but a few days, or an old man who does not live out his years; the one who dies at a hundred will be thought a mere child."

These passages describe a time of peace, prosperity, and longevity, conditions unique to the millennial reign.

Cultural and Technological Flourishing

The Millennium was a time of incredible advancement and creativity. Guided by the wisdom of Christ and His saints, humanity flourished in areas such as art, architecture, health, and technology.

- **Art and Architecture**: Inspired by divine principles, artists and builders created awe-inspiring works of beauty and grandeur. Cities became centers of innovation, reflecting the glory of God in their design. I believe much of the stunning art from the past, such as Michelangelo's Sistine Chapel, could have been created by resurrected saints or even angels, with their contributions later attributed to human names (for example, Archangel Michael becoming Michelangelo).
- **Health and Healing**: Advances in health were facilitated through water, sound cymatics, music, and the use of bells. These techniques, rooted in divine wisdom, promoted physical, mental, and spiritual well-being.
- **Peace and Prosperity**: While it cannot be stated with absolute certainty, I believe that the number of wars recorded in our history books during this time may have been greatly exaggerated, and that nations likely experienced much more peace under Christ's rule. Rain fell in its season for those who worshiped the King rightly, ensuring abundant harvests and economic prosperity.

- **Free Energy**: Harnessing principles of divine order, energy was abundant and free, eliminating the struggles and inequalities caused by limited resources.

Distinct from the New Heavens and Earth

It is essential to distinguish life in the Millennium from life in the new heavens and new earth—which is what we are hoping for today. While the Millennium was marked by Christ's reign and the presence of sin among mortals, the new creation described in Isaiah 11:6-9 and Revelation 21-22 will be completely free from sin, death, and the influence of Satan, fallen angels and demons.

- In the new creation, the lion (or wolf, take your pick) will lie down with the lamb, and children will play safely with vipers (Isaiah 11:6-8).
- The former things will have passed away, and God will dwell with His people in perfect harmony (Revelation 21:3-4).

Life in the Millennium was a unique era of divine governance, cultural flourishing, and spiritual accountability. While it was a time of peace and prosperity under Christ's rule, the presence of sin among mortals highlighted humanity's continued need for redemption and rigid governance (rod of iron). Nevertheless, the Millennium was a testament to Christ's authority and the transformative power of His Kingdom, setting the stage for the final, eternal reign of God in the coming new heavens and new earth—just after Satan's little season.

Okay, If These Things Are So, Then... *Who the Heck Are We?!*

Following an understandable initial disappointment, one of the most common questions raised by believers when presented with this evidence concerns our identity *today*. If the second coming of Christ has already occurred, and we are not destined for life during the Millennium, who then are we? And what remains of our "blessed hope"?

Revelation 20:5 states, *"But the rest of the dead lived not again until the thousand years were finished."* This passage, loaded with implications, offers fertile ground for much conjecture, especially within the framework of Satan's little season theology. Who exactly are these "rest of the dead," and could their identity have any bearing on us today?

The "rest of the dead" in this verse seem to stand in contrast to those who partake in the *first resurrection*—the saints who reigned with Christ during the Millennial Kingdom (Revelation 20:4)—numbered as 144,000. These individuals are described as blessed and holy, reigning as priests and kings alongside Christ. But the rest of humanity—those who were not part of this first resurrection—appear to have been left to live normal human lives, albeit blessed, or in a state of waiting until the end of the thousand years.

If Satan's little season is understood as our current age, i.e. post-Millennium, then it raises a provocative question: Are we the "rest of the dead" who have come to life again during this period?

Descendants of the Rest of the Dead

Another possibility is that we are *descendants* of these "rest of the dead." If the Millennial Kingdom was marked by unparalleled peace and prosperity, and if its rulers were the resurrected saints, it stands to reason that the "rest of the dead" could include those who later repopulated the earth, whether by natural means or through more extraordinary methods.

Some alternative theories even propose that much of humanity today might not descend from natural lineage but from mysterious origins, such as "cabbage patch" babies or incubator babies (more on those later). These speculative ideas suggest that entire populations may have been either non-traditionally or artificially created, or repopulated in a post-Millennial era. Could these theories connect with the "rest of the dead," implying that humanity was resurrected or recreated in some unnatural way after the Millennium? Some have even suggested that cabbage patch babies were brought into being by God himself, as an unorthodox means of resurrecting the rest of the dead and repopulating the earth after the post Millenium vacancy.

While such ideas may lack direct biblical support, they provoke fascinating questions about the means by which life might have continued or restarted after the events described in Revelation.

A further layer of speculation involves the possibility of cloning or genetic manipulation through baby incubators found on Coney Island and at various World Fairs (more on those later). If Satan's little season is a time of unparalleled deception, it is conceivable that the rulers of this age, under Satan's influence, might resort to creating life through unnatural means. This could align with broader themes of rebellion against God's order and manipulation of His creation, further underscoring the darkness of this period.

How Then Should We Live?

Okay, so, if we are the rest of the dead, their descendants, or products of some post-Millennial re-creation, it fundamentally changes how we view our identity and purpose, doesn't it? Rather than awaiting a future Millennial reign, we seem called to wrestle with the spiritual realities of Satan's little season. Our "blessed hope" may lie not in a second coming that has already occurred, but in living faithfully amid a world marked by deception, awaiting the final, eternal judgment, victory, and the renewal of all things in the new heavens and new earth. That doesn't seem so bad, does it?

Furthermore, no matter how we came to be, one thing remains certain: as human beings we are redeemable still. Christ is still King, and by His stripes, we are healed.

This perspective reframes our identity and mission. It challenges us to consider what it means to live as faithful and effective witnesses in a time when the past is obscured and the future remains uncertain.

While establishing a timeline is always daunting and, in the end, too risky, I believe that a general approximation, such as pictured above, can give a very sound idea of the biblical timeline, and a better idea of the times we live in.

CHAPTER 3

Lucifer-Satan: The Self-Styled Light- Bringer

"To you, Sovereign Grand Inspectors General, we say this, that you may repeat it, to the Brethren of the 32nd, 31st and 30th degrees. The Masonic religion should be, by all of us, initiates of the high degrees, maintained in the purity of the Luciferian Doctrine. Yes! Lucifer is God, and the true and pure religion is the belief in Lucifer."

~Albert Pike, 33rd Degree Master Mason and author of the Masonic doctrinal blueprint: *Morals and Dogma*, when he addressed the 23rd Supreme Council of the world on July 14, 1889.

Throughout history, there has been a recurring theme of satanic inversion—where truth is twisted into falsehood, light into darkness, and vice versa. This pattern reflects a profound aspect of Satan's nature: his penchant for inversion and deception. A closer examination of his tactics reveals how these inversions manifest in historical periods and cultural shifts.

What's in a Name?

The term "Satan" derives from the Hebrew word שָׂטָן (satan), meaning "adversary," "accuser," or "opponent." It first appears in the Hebrew Bible, where it is used both as a title and as a description of an oppositional role. In its earliest usages, "satan" is not always a proper name but rather a functional title, referring to someone who opposes or obstructs. For instance, in Numbers 22:22, the angel of the Lord acts as a "satan" against Balaam, standing in his way as an adversary—blocking him. In the book of Job (Job 1:6-12; 2:1-7), "Satan" is depicted as a heavenly being who serves as an accuser, challenging Job's faithfulness before God.

In later Hebraic and Christian traditions, the term evolved to refer specifically to a singular being—an arch-enemy of God and humanity. This development can be seen in texts like 1 Chronicles 21:1, where Satan is directly linked to tempting David to sin, and in the New Testament, where Satan is described as the tempter, the deceiver, and the ruler of this world (Matthew 4:1-11; John 12:31; Revelation 12:9). Here, Satan transitions from a functional adversary to a personal being symbolizing evil and opposition to God.

Biblically, Satan's role is multifaceted. As an accuser, Satan seeks to expose human sin (Zechariah 3:1-2) and undermine God's creation. As a deceiver, he spreads lies and falsehoods to lead humanity astray (John 8:44; 2 Corinthians 11:14). These actions underline his unrelenting mission to challenge God's authority and distort His plans for salvation. This adversarial role cements Satan's identity as the ultimate opposition to divine goodness and truth.

Lucifer: The Light-Bringer in Name and Legacy

The name *Lucifer* also carries profound etymological and symbolic significance. Derived from the Latin *lucifer*, meaning "light-bringer" or "light-bearer," the term is traditionally linked to the Hebrew word *helel,* found in Isaiah 14:12. In this passage, the prophet mocks the downfall of the Babylonian king, referring to him as the "morning star," a figure that Christian tradition later associated with the fallen angel who became Satan. The name *Lucifer* thus evokes the paradox of a being once radiant, now fallen—a former herald of divine illumination turned into a corrupter of truth.

Lucifer: Father of the Enlightenment

The Enlightenment, an intellectual movement of the 17th and 18th centuries, is often celebrated for its emphasis on reason, scientific inquiry, and the pursuit of knowledge. Yet, its philosophical undercurrents sometimes strayed into rebellion against established religious authority and traditional morality. Lucifer, as the archetypal "light-bringer," can be seen as a symbolic figurehead of this era—a paradoxical patron of illumination that casts shadows. Like the Enlightenment thinkers, who sought to "enlighten" humanity with new ideas, Lucifer's legacy is one of a being who offers knowledge but at great cost, echoing the temptation in Eden: "You shall be as gods, knowing good and evil" (Genesis 3:5).

Lucifer: Father of the Illuminati

The Illuminati, a secretive group associated with esoteric knowledge and power, takes its name from the Latin word for "the enlightened ones." This title resonates with the concept of Lucifer as the light-bearer, a being who offers illumination but often leads astray. While historical accounts of the Illuminati portray it as a group seeking to challenge oppressive systems, conspiracy theories have painted it as a shadowy force manipulating global events. The link between Lucifer and the Illuminati lies in their shared symbolic association with hidden knowledge, enlightenment, and power—a reminder of the dual-edged nature of enlightenment that can both liberate and corrupt.

Satan's Imprisonment and the "Dark Ages"

Satan's imprisonment in the bottomless pit, as described in Revelation 20, represents a period of enforced darkness for him. During this millennium, when Satan was bound and unable to deceive the nations, the period that followed was named "The Dark Ages." This nomenclature is deeply ironic and revealing, as it were. Remember, he was chained and imprisoned in a pit, which was probably quite dark. So, in hindsight, those were dark ages all right—but for him alone.

The "Dark Ages"

The term "Dark Ages" was coined to describe the time between the fall of the Roman Empire and the beginning of the Renaissance (roughly 476 AD up until around 1000 AD). This period was characterized by a perceived lack of cultural and scientific progress, a darkness that obscured the light of knowledge and enlightenment. The choice of this term reflects a subtle yet profound inversion: what should have been a period of growth and illumination following the defeat of evil was instead cast in terms of darkness and ignorance. So, by labeling this period as "dark," the satanic narrative serves to obscure the truth about the spiritual state of the world and the genuine progress of humanity during this time. It creates a perception of a lost era, overshadowed by ignorance and superstition, conveniently ignoring the contributions and developments that occurred under Christ's rule.

The Enlightenment and Satan's Self-Styled Role

Upon Satan's release from the pit, the period known as the Enlightenment emerged, characterized by a seeming explosion of intellectual and scientific advancements. This era marked a shift from religious and dogmatic thinking to an emphasis on reason, science, and empirical evidence. This is no coincidence. With the binding of Satan during the Millennium, the world had been operating under divine order, with Christ's reign restraining the influence of deception and chaos. However, as Satan was loosed, his deceptive influence began to creep into human thought, particularly in the realm of intellectual pursuits.

The Enlightenment can be seen as a strategic move by Satan to subvert the spiritual order that had existed during the Millennial reign. By promoting reason and scientific progress as the primary tools for understanding the world, Satan sought to dethrone God and replace divine authority with human intellect. This period fostered a spirit of skepticism and challenged long-held religious beliefs, particularly Christianity. It ushered in the rise of secularism and laid the groundwork for ideologies that would later fuel the French Revolution, the rise of atheism, and the rejection of traditional religious values.

Key Enlightenment figures, such as Voltaire, Rousseau, and Kant, to name just a few, advocated for the autonomy of human reason, often at the expense of faith. This intellectual rebellion against established norms can be viewed as part of Satan's plan to lead humanity astray, encouraging the idea that human understanding, rather than divine revelation, should dictate truth. The emphasis on empirical evidence and skepticism toward spiritual realities fit perfectly within the narrative of Satan's self-styled role as the one who would deceive the nations, leading them into the false belief that their own intellects were sufficient to discern truth without the need for divine guidance.

As the Enlightenment flourished, so did the undercurrents of spiritual blindness, as the supernatural and the divine were relegated to the margins of human understanding. This philosophical shift was not merely a cultural movement, but a spiritual one, with Satan positioning himself as the ultimate "enlightener," offering false wisdom to humanity in place of the true light that comes from God. Thus, the Enlightenment served as both a symptom and a catalyst of the broader spiritual deception unfolding during Satan's little season.

A False Light of Freedom

In 1886, France gifted the United States with the Statue of Liberty—a symbol celebrated as a beacon of freedom and democracy. However, some interpretations of the oddly hermaphrodite-looking statue suggest this figure may not represent "Lady Liberty" but rather Lucifer, or the light-bearer. This statue, towering with a broken chain at its feet, is said to portray freedom, but may also symbolize a release from some divine bondage; Satan chained and thrown in the pit, perhaps? Further, "Lady" Liberty's appearance has distinctively masculine traits, evoking the hermaphroditic symbolism often associated with occult and esoteric depictions of Satan—such as the goat-like Baphomet. The date inscribed on her tablet, July 4, 1776, aligns with the founding of both the United States and the Illuminati, pointing to an era when secret societies and occult knowledge sought to influence the direction of human enlightenment and freedom. Seen in this light, the statue becomes a potent symbol, not of divine liberty, but of Lucifer's influence over the New World.

A side-by-side comparison of a painting titled *Satan Summoning His Legions* (our cover) and "Lady" Liberty. Same dude, different drag.

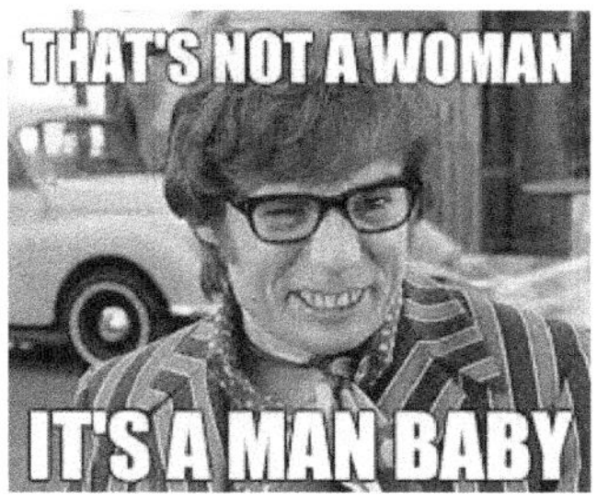

What happened on this date: July IV, MDCCLXXVI (July 4th, 1776), other than what we've been told?

Many don't know that the broken chain at the foot of the Statue of Liberty may also represent Satan's chains being broken off after one thousand years in the pit.

The Subtle Craft of Deception

Satan's ability to invert truth and manipulate historical narratives highlights his craftiness and his role as the master deceiver. By controlling how history is perceived and how enlightenment is defined, he seeks to mislead and confuse.

- **Historical Narratives:** The portrayal of historical periods such as the Dark Ages and the Enlightenment serves as a tool for Satan's deception. By framing these eras in terms of darkness and light, he influences perceptions and attitudes towards spiritual and intellectual matters.
- **Cultural and Religious Impact:** The inversion of truth affects not only historical narratives but also

contemporary cultural and religious beliefs. By promoting secularism and skepticism as forms of enlightenment, Satan aims to undermine faith and spiritual understanding.

Satan's inversion of truth—from the "Dark Ages" to the "Enlightenment"—reflects a deliberate and cunning strategy to manipulate human perception and spiritual understanding. By turning light into darkness and vice versa, he aims to obscure divine truth and lead humanity astray, all while presenting himself as a benefactor of knowledge and enlightenment.

CHAPTER 4:

How The Devil's Minions Took Over

"Again, the devil taketh him up into an exceeding high mountain, and sheweth him all the kingdoms of the world, and the glory of them; And saith unto him, All these things will I give thee, if thou wilt fall down and worship me."
~Matthew 4:8-9

In John 8:44, Jesus reveals a chilling truth when He confronts the religious leaders of His time, saying: *"You are of your father the devil, and the desires of your father you want to do."* This powerful statement suggests that Satan, not only as a spiritual being but as a literal progenitor, has a seedline on earth. Jesus' words imply that there are individuals who are spiritually, perhaps even physically, descended from Satan. They share his nature, desires, and ultimately, his agenda. These individuals—whom we may call the "children of the devil" or "Satan's kids"—are not merely symbolic figures but part of a more tangible lineage, carrying on his work of deception, corruption, and rebellion.

It is within this context that we must consider the idea that Satan, upon his release for the "little season" mentioned in Revelation 20:3-7, has made a pact with these descendants—those he has aligned with his cause—whether physically, spiritually, or both. Much like the temptation in Matthew 4, where Satan offers Christ the kingdoms of the world in exchange for worship, Satan extends a similar offer to his earthly followers. In exchange for loyalty and service to his cause, he grants them power, wealth, and dominance over the systems of the world. This pact solidifies their status as rulers of finance, politics, and society—tools through which they advance Satan's agenda.

The Ruling Class, who represent a significant portion of this satanic bloodline, hold an undeniably high concentration of wealth and influence despite constituting only a small percentage of the global population. While they make up approximately only a fragment of the world's population, they hold a disproportionately high share of the world's wealth. For example, the infamous thirteen Illuminati families, as listed by Fritz Springmeier in his 1995 book: *The Top 13 Illuminati Bloodlines,* control a substantial portion of global finance, with prominent names like the Rothschilds, Rockefeller, and others at the helm of some of the world's largest banks and financial institutions. According to some estimates, these people control roughly 40-50% of global financial capital, particularly in banking, media, and investment sectors, despite their small population size-ratio.

This immense concentration of wealth and power is not a coincidence.

During Satan's "little season," his earthly children now thrive. The networks of influence they have built over the last centuries allow them to maintain control over key industries like media, education, real estate, and finance. Their grip on these industries enables them to shape global events, influence governments, and direct the flow of capital in ways that align with their agenda—an agenda rooted in deception, rebellion, and opposition to God's Kingdom.

This pact with Satan, while offering immense power and control in the present age, is ultimately part of his broader plan to unify the world against Christ in the final battle. The wealth and influence wielded by Satan's seedline may give them dominance in this "little season," but their reign is temporary. The ultimate defeat of Satan and his seedline will come at the very end of all things, when Christ establishes His eternal Kingdom, and new heaven and a new earth, and brings justice to all who have aligned themselves with the forces of darkness.

Who are the 13 Illuminati families?

1. The Astor Bloodline

2. The Bundy Bloodline

3. The Collins Bloodline

4. The DuPont Bloodline

5. The Freeman Bloodline

6. The Kennedy Bloodline

7. The Li Bloodline

8. The Onassis Bloodline

9. The Rockefeller Bloodline

10. The Russell Bloodline

11. The Van Duyn Bloodline

12. The Merovingian Bloodline

13. The Rothschild Bloodline

According to Fritz Springmeier, listed above are *The Top 13 Illuminati Bloodlines. There are others, of course, but these would be the most influential.*

Satan's Seduction of the Elite

In Matthew 4:8-9, we read about one of the most pivotal moments in the life of Jesus Christ, where Satan attempts to tempt Him with an offer of earthly power and influence:

"Again, the devil took Him up on an exceedingly high mountain, and showed Him all the kingdoms of the world and their glory. And he said to Him, 'All these things I will give You if You will fall down and worship me.'" ~Matthew 4:8-9, NKJV

This passage encapsulates Satan's core strategy: to offer power, wealth, and dominion over the earth in exchange for allegiance. Note how Christ doesn't object to the devil's claim that he owns it all. However, Christ, steadfast in His mission and righteousness, rejects this temptation, affirming that worship belongs to God alone. He resists the allure of worldly power, choosing instead to follow His divine purpose and secure eternal victory through His obedience to the Father.

In stark contrast, after Christ's Millennial rule, once Satan is released from the pit in the final stages of history, we see a different outcome. Satan's strategy does not end with Christ but is redirected to certain people and families, particularly those with deep connections to the Jewish elite, such as the Rothschilds and other prominent banking families. These families, through their vast wealth and manipulation of global finance, education, real estate, and government, became key players in the establishment of what some call *The Synagogue of Satan*—a dark alliance, Jewish at its core, of Masons, Jesuits, dark occultists, and many others working in concert to consolidate power and control over the world's systems.

Jesus is the one who originally coined *the Synagogue of Satan* in Revelation 2:9 and 3:9, when He said,

"I know thy works, and tribulation, and poverty, (but thou art rich) and I know the blasphemy of them which say they are Jews, and are not, but are the synagogue of Satan."
~Revelation 2:9

"Behold, I will make them of the synagogue of Satan, which say they are Jews, and are not, but do lie; behold, I will make them to come and worship before thy feet, and to know that I have loved thee." ~Revelation 3:9

These deceptive individuals, families, and organizations, who falsely present themselves as "God's chosen people," have wielded financial influence for centuries. During Jesus' time, they controlled synagogues and religious institutions. Throughout the Millennium, however, they operated in secrecy, fully aware that under Christ and His saints' rule, they held no real power. Hidden in the shadows, they plotted and schemed for generations, preparing for the moment Satan would be released. Now, in their father's little season, they have re-emerged and gained control over society.

When Satan was "loosed for a little season" as prophesied in Revelation 20:7-10, his influence extended not only to individuals but to entire systems and nations. His promises of power and dominion, once firmly rejected by Christ, found fertile ground among these wicked people. Unlike Christ, who resisted the devil's offer, these satanic bloodlines, driven by greed and an insatiable thirst for control and power, showing the same lusts as their father, eagerly aligned themselves with his plan. Just as it happened during Christ's temptation in Matthew 4, Satan whispered to them, offering them all the kingdoms of the world in exchange for worship and loyalty.

In the case of the Rothschilds, who became infamous for their domination of global banking and finance, their rise to power coincided with Satan's offer. These families, and others like them, not only accumulated vast wealth but also infiltrated the institutions that shape the modern world: education, government, finance, and media. Through strategic control of the financial system, they manipulated economies and established a cycle of debt that ensured their continued dominance. Their grip on education and government institutions solidified their influence, shaping policy and controlling the narrative through media manipulation and political influence.

The Rise of the Dark Occultist Rulers

Indeed, the world is ruled by psychopathic dark occultists and satanists. To be clear, however, the word "occult" or "occultist" simply means "hidden," as does the term "esoteric." So, at its core, the study of *the occult* involves uncovering and understanding things that are concealed or not readily apparent. There is nothing inherently wrong with researching and/or reading about the occult, as it is essentially the pursuit of deeper knowledge and truth. In fact, Solomon, the wisest man in the Bible, reminds us of the value of such pursuits in Proverbs 25:2: *"It is the glory of God to conceal a thing: but the honour of kings is to search out a matter."* So, the act of seeking *hidden truths* can be noble and God-honoring when done with the right heart and intent.

However, a clear line must be drawn when it comes to "dark occultism," which involves seeking hidden knowledge and power through forbidden means such as magick, demons, and spirits. This path is not only dangerous but explicitly condemned in Scripture (Exodus 22:18; Deuteronomy 18:11–12; Leviticus 19:26; Leviticus 20:27; 1 Samuel 15:23), as it opens doors to deception, manipulation, and much spiritual harm. The rulers of this dark age willfully and knowingly engage in such practices. They seize power through dark occultism to control, dominate, demonize, curse and exploit mankind. Their reliance on these forbidden practices demonstrates their perversion and betray their dark allegiance.

This The Ruling Class network of high-ranking dark occultists is said to include not only Jewish families like the Rothschilds but also a wide range of Masonic orders, Jesuits, and other secret societies and occult organizations, forming an intricate web of those who secretly control the world's institutions. These families and organizations work together to consolidate power, shaping global events to their benefit while maintaining an air of legitimacy. They operate covertly, masquerading and acting as benefactors, businessmen, politicians, or worse... religious leaders.

The term "Synagogue of Satan" refers to a group that outwardly claims to be aligned with God's people but is, in fact, deeply entrenched in sin and rebellion. Christianity has not been exempt from their methods of infiltration and control.

Their influence, now centuries old, is evident in the architecture of global power. Whether in the form of the Freemasons, who wield immense influence in politics and society, or other secret societies, who have had a significant impact on education and missionary work, these secret societies are part of a larger system that perpetuates Satan's dominion over the world.

Furthering their Grip on Society

The true power of the ruling class is seen in their control over key aspects of modern society. Education has long been a tool of manipulation, with these people infiltrating institutions to shape the values and beliefs of future generations. By controlling the flow of information and dictating what is taught, they ensure that the narrative remains aligned with their goals, reinforcing it through the next generation.

In real estate, they have amassed vast amounts of property, ensuring that they control the land upon which the world operates. By doing so, they exert influence over cities, nations, and even entire continents.

Even though the bible warns of such activities in Isaiah 5: 8-9: *"Woe unto them that join house to house, that lay field to field, till there be no place, that they may be placed alone in the midst of the earth! In mine ears said the Lord of hosts, of a truth many houses shall be desolate, even great and fair, without inhabitant."*

They care not of righteousness or of God's warnings. They still amass land upon land, and are never satisfied.

In finance, they hold the reins of the world's economic systems, orchestrating economic booms and busts to keep nations indebted and dependent on their control. As for the arts, it is a well observed fact that they hold a tight monopoly in Hollywood—pulling the strings over which artists, movies, and actors meet with success and are promoted for more. Mel Gibson knows it, and now you know it.

These Satan worshippers infiltrated every facet of society and strengthening their grip on power. However, as history unfolds and prophecy nears its fulfillment, the ultimate triumph will belong to Christ. The Synagogue of Satan, despite its power and influence, will ultimately be exposed and brought to ruin as Christ's final and eternal reign is established.

In Satan's Little Season, they became the owners, the rulers, the wealthy, the builders, the founders, etc. They went by many names across the centuries: the Oddfellows, the Freemasons, the Illuminati, etc. Today, we also know them as the 1%, The Ruling Class, the Controllers, The World Economic Forum, the Hidden Government, the Secret Government, the Hellfire Club, and the name we are forbidden to speak that rhymes with *news*. But, the Bible, God's Holy Word, is less courteous when referring to "they", "them". Indeed, in Scripture they are often referred to as *unclean animals*, such as serpents and/or dogs.

Brood of Vipers

In the New Testament, John the Baptist and the Lord Jesus Christ referred to these deceitful people as a "brood of vipers" (Matthew 3:7; Matthew 12:34; Matthew 23:33). The term "serpents" carries profound biblical significance, linking these individuals to the very nature of Satan himself, who is first introduced as a serpent in Genesis 3:1-15 and later identified as "that old serpent, called the devil, and Satan" in Revelation 12:9 and 20:2.

Jesus, in John 8:44, explicitly identified these individuals as *children of the devil*, stating that they carry out the desires of their father, who was "a murderer from the beginning" and "the father of lies." This lineage of deceit, violence, and rebellion against God positions them as a literal brood of vipers— offspring of the serpent.

Today, during Satan's Little Season, these same "serpents" continue their wicked ways, thriving in deception and leading many astray. They wield influence over institutions, spread lies, and perpetuate spiritual blindness, furthering the devil's agenda in his brief season of power.

Outside Are the Dogs

Again, in the New Testament, the term "dogs" is used metaphorically in a few different ways, often to refer to people who are considered outsiders, unclean, or morally corrupt, especially in relation to the Israelites of old. Here are some notable instances:

1. **Matthew 7:6**: "Do not give what is holy to the *dogs*, and do not throw your pearls before *pigs*, lest they trample them underfoot and turn and tear you to pieces."

    o   In this context, "dogs" are people who reject the wisdom or message of the gospel, likened to animals who don't appreciate the value of holy things.

2. **Philippians 3:2**: "Look out for the *dogs*, look out for the *evil workers*, look out for those *who mutilate the flesh*."

    o   Paul uses "dogs" to describe people who are false teachers, particularly those who insist on rabbinical circumcision (the "Judaizers"). It refers to those who are corrupt and spiritually dangerous.

3. **Revelation 22:15**: "Outside are the *dogs* and *sorcerers* and the sexually immoral and murderers and idolaters, and *everyone who loves and practices falsehood*."

    o   Here, "dogs" symbolize those who are excluded from the heavenly city, representing people who live in sin and rejection of God's ways.

In each of these cases, "dogs" refers to those outside of God's covenant, often with a focus on people who are spiritually defiled, unclean, wicked, or directly opposed to God's message and kingdom.

Jesus and the Canaanite Woman

In Matthew 15:22-28 (and Mark 7:27-28), Jesus famously encounters a Canaanite woman who begs for mercy on behalf of her demon-possessed daughter. Initially, Jesus responds by calling her a "dog," a term that echoes the biblical disdain for certain people, who were seen as a spiritually, and perhaps even physically, unclean. Jesus' words seem harsh, but they underline the idea of spiritual impurity and exclusion. He states:

" It is not meet to take the children's bread, and to cast it to dogs." ~Matthew 15:26

While Jesus ultimately graciously heals the woman's daughter after her humble reply, this interaction establishes a precedent for certain people being referred to as "dogs." In this case, the Canaanites, due to their idolatry and spiritual rebellion, were considered outside of God's covenant. This identification with "dogs" is not only a rebuke but a powerful symbol of exclusion. It highlights a boundary between the covenant people of Israel and those seen as unclean or rebellious.

Throughout history, there have been numerous occasions where individuals considered unclean—such as moneylenders, parasitic groups, and satanists—were expelled from various Western nations. Each of these events serves as a powerful historical reflection of divine exclusion.

According to researcher Andrew Carrington Hitchcock, author of *The Synagogue of Satan*, these people, most Jewish in origin, were mass-expelled from various countries, sometimes multiple times, over the course of history. The list of these historical expulsions includes:

1. **Mainz, 1012**
2. **France, 1182**
3. **Upper Bavaria, 1276**
4. **England, 1290**
5. **France, 1306**
6. **Saxony, 1349**
7. **Hungary, 1360**
8. **Belgium, 1370**
9. **France, 1394**
10. **Austria, 1420**
11. **Lyons, 1420**
12. **Cologne, 1424**
13. **Mainz, 1438**
14. **Augsburg, 1438**
15. **Upper Bavaria, 1442**
16. **Lithuania, 1495**
17. **Portugal, 1496**
18. **Spain, 1492**
19. **Italy, 1492**
20. **Prussia, 1510**
21. **Prague, 1541**
22. **Papal States, 1569**
23. **Vienna, 1669**
24. **Slovakia, 1744**
25. **Moscow, 1891**

This extensive list shows the repeated expulsions and rejections faced by Satan's children (John 8:44). Note also, how these expulsions happened mainly during the *"dark ages"* and Renaissance era, i.e. during the Millenium. Indeed, these are the very centuries that would have coincided with the Millenium of Christ. So, the Lord wasn't playing when He said in Revelation, speaking of His kingdom, *"outside are the dogs"* (Revelation 22.15).

Hitchcock notes that these expulsions were not limited to one nation or culture but were widespread throughout Europe, the West, and beyond.

These repeated expulsions point to an undeniable pattern of divine judgment and exclusion, especially during the Millenium, aligning with the idea that these estranged people, always wandering—those who have rejected Christ—are like "dogs", spiritually unclean and not welcomed into the Kingdom of God.

The Ruler's Emancipation and Dominion

The concept of the Ruling Class's emancipation and their subsequent rise to financial and mediatic dominance in Western nations can be viewed through a spiritual lens, particularly in the context of Satan's Little Season. This pivotal event, which probably began around 1776—a year marked by revolutionary upheavals such as the founding of the Bavarian Illuminati and the Declaration of Independence—coincides with a broader shift in global power structures and societal values.

Historically, these satanic bloodlines were often confined to specific roles, such as moneylending and trade, due to severe restrictions placed on them by Christian-dominated societies. However, with the "Enlightenment" and the gradual secularization of Europe, barriers to their participation in broader societal and economic spheres began to erode. This period of emancipation opened doors for their parasitic influence to expand significantly into areas like finance, media, and political propaganda. Over time, this influence grew exponentially, with key families establishing their unprecedented control over everything.

From this perspective, The Ruling Class's dominance in media and finance serves as a mechanism to propagate ideas and values that undermine traditional Christian morality and societal structures. Through decades-long control of narratives and economic systems, they have been instrumental in fostering materialism, secularism, and moral relativism—ideologies linked to Satan's agenda of leading nations astray. This process has been gradual, yes, but unrelenting. This dominance aligns with a scriptural warning of Satan's temporary reign and his use of worldly power to subvert God's kingdom on earth—his little season.

Twice the Children of Hell

"Woe unto you, scribes and Pharisees, hypocrites! For ye compass sea and land to make one proselyte [convert], and when he is made, ye make him twofold more the child of hell than yourselves." ~Matthew 23:15

In Matthew 23:15, Jesus delivers a scathing rebuke to the scribes and Pharisees, calling them "hypocrites" and condemning their efforts to recruit new pawns to join their ranks. He says, *"Ye compass sea and land to make one proselyte, and when he is made, ye make him twofold more the child of hell than yourselves."* This verse holds a profound connection to the way the satanic elite recruit individuals to join their ranks—through carefully constructed covenants, rituals, pacts, and secret societies, designed to strengthen their grip on power and deceive others into doing their bidding.

These secretive covenants, operating in the shadows of our world, target individuals from all walks of life—artists, educators, media personalities, politicians, and more. Through a combination of manipulation, promises of fame and fortune, and even coercion, they draw these individuals into a world where they must abandon their morals and serve the dark forces of Satan. Much like the Pharisees in the time of Jesus, these "recruits" are led to believe they are joining an elite group, but in reality, they are bound to serve the purpose of a far more sinister agenda.

The recruitment process often begins with the allure of power. Those seeking wealth, influence, or fame are approached with the opportunity to join these secret organizations—often cloaked in the guise of exclusive clubs or high-status circles. The price, however, is high: they must swear a blood oath, allegiance to Satan, and in doing so, make a pact that binds them to his cause. These individuals become pawns in the larger game, infiltrating the key spheres of society such as the arts, education, and media.

Through these infiltrations, the satanic ruling class extend their reach, using their recruits to influence public opinion, control narratives, and advance ideologies that undermine traditional values, Christian morality, and societal order. The influence of these individuals becomes far-reaching, as they are now driven to recruit others, perpetuating the cycle of deception. As Jesus warned, once these individuals are coerced, they become "twofold more the child of hell," as each new recruit further distorts the world and makes it more difficult for others to see the truth. The entertainment industry is perhaps the most overt and obvious result of what this actually looks like.

It's a Big Club

Around a decade ago, singer-songwriter Altiyan Childs, winner of Australia's "X Factor," released a 5-hour video in which he boldly exposed the ongoing satanic deception within the entertainment industry. According to Childs, entertainers in music, TV, and film are promised fame and fortune in exchange for their loyalty to Satan, to The Ruling Class—and their silence. In the video, which you may be able to view here, he reveals how these individuals are united in this deception and how they can be identified through their masonic signs and signals: https://rumble.com/v3hpb22-x-factor-winner-reveals-worlds-secret-religion-altiyan-childs.html

The Bible says, *"A naughty person, a wicked man, walketh with a froward mouth. He winketh with his eyes, he speaketh with his feet, he teacheth with his fingers; perverseness is in his heart, he deviseth mischief continually; he soweth discord."* ~Proverbs 6:12-14

The late stand-up comedian George Carlin also used his platform to expose Satan's minions. He is famously remembered for saying, *"It's a BIG club, and you ain't in it."* While the text of his speech below contains profanity (reader discretion is advised), I believe the excerpt is important and worth sharing here.

"But there's a reason. There's a reason. There's a reason for this, there's a reason education sucks, and it's the same reason that it will never, ever, ever be fixed. It's never gonna get any better. Don't look for it. Be happy with what you got. Because the owners of this country don't want that. I'm talking about the real owners now, the real owners, the big wealthy business interests that control things and make all the important decisions. Forget the politicians. The politicians are put there to give you the idea that you have freedom of choice. You don't. You have no choice. You have owners. They own you. They own everything. They own all the important land. They own

*and control the corporations. They've long since bought and paid for the senate, the congress, the state houses, the city halls, they got the judges in their back pockets and they own all the big media companies so they control just about all of the news and information you get to hear. They got you by the b****. They spend billions of dollars every year lobbying, lobbying, to get what they want. Well, we know what they want. They want more for themselves and less for everybody else, but I'll tell you what they don't want: They don't want a population of citizens capable of critical thinking. They don't want well-informed, well-educated people capable of critical thinking. They're not interested in that. That doesn't help them. That's against their interests. Right. They don't want people who are smart enough to sit around a kitchen table to figure out how badly they're getting f***** by a system that threw them overboard 30 f****** years ago. They don't want that. You know what they want? They want obedient workers. Obedient workers. People who are just smart enough to run the machines and do the paperwork, and just dumb enough to passively accept all these increasingly s***** jobs with the lower pay, the longer hours, the reduced benefits, the end of overtime and the vanishing pension that disappears the minute you go to collect it, and now they're coming for your Social Security money. They want your retirement money. They want it back so they can give it to their criminal friends on Wall Street, and you know something? They'll get it. They'll get it all from you, sooner or later, 'cause they own this f****** place. It's a big club, and you ain't in it. You and I are not in the big club. And by the way, it's the same big club they use to beat you over the head with all day long when they tell you what to believe. All day long beating you over the head in their media telling you what to believe, what to think and what to buy. The table is tilted folks. The game is rigged, and nobody seems to notice, nobody seems to care. Good honest hard-*

*working people—white collar, blue collar, it doesn't matter what color shirt you have on—good honest hard-working people continue—these are people of modest means—continue to elect these rich c********** who don't give a f*** about them. They don't give a f*** about you. They don't give a f*** about you. They don't care about you at all—at all—at all. And nobody seems to notice, nobody seems to care. That's what the owners count on; the fact that Americans will probably remain willfully ignorant of the big red, white and blue d*** that's being jammed up their a** everyday. Because the owners of this country know the truth: it's called the American Dream, because you have to be asleep to believe it."*

George Carlin nailed it that day. Indeed, in Satan's little season, the people who are really in control are in one BIG club. And you and I aren't in it. We can be thankful for that. And we can rest assured that their whole operation of deception won't last. The truth is coming out from many different sources. They are being exposed, gradually, truthfully, and boldly. Praise Yahweh!

Comedian George Carlin, along with many others, tried to warn us.

Whether they hide their one eye or hush their lips (it's a secret, after all), these pics show us how these entertainers know the secret cabal—and are part of it. Here's a hint: If they have a big platform, you can be sure it's not by accident.

CHAPTER 5:

Tartaria? Or Remains of the Millenium?

"For the stone shall cry out of the wall, and the beam out of the timber shall answer it. Woe to him that buildeth a town with blood, and establisheth a city by iniquity!"
~Habakkuk, 2:11-12

"I tell you," He replied, "if they keep quiet, the stones will cry out."
~Jesus Christ, (Luke 19:40)

In this chapter, we delve into the fascinating possibility that many of the ancient buildings and architectural wonders scattered across the earth may not simply be relics of long-lost civilizations, but rather remnants of the Millennium described in Scripture. As we explore these structures—many of which defy conventional historical explanations—we'll consider the idea that they might not belong to forgotten empires, such as Tartaria, but rather represent the remains of a world that once thrived under the reign of Christ. Could these buildings hold clues to a forgotten era, one that was overshadowed by the rise of new powers and narratives? Let's examine the evidence and explore how the ancient world's architectural legacy might reveal more than we ever imagined.

From the grand cathedrals and European castles to the magnificent state capitols and parliament buildings found in nearly every state and province, and even to orphanages, convents, high schools, and insane asylums, we are surrounded by marvelous ancient structures in our cities. Yet, most of us have never taken the time to question the history behind what we admire. These buildings are architectural wonders, to say the least.

It is only when we delve into their origins that we begin to uncover discrepancies in the accepted narrative. In most cases, the stories surrounding these structures are built on common and repetitive themes:

- These buildings were all "founded" rather than built.
- Their supposed conception and construction were completed in record time during an era with very limited technology (horse and buggy, chisel and hammer).
- The structures we see today are invariably second or third iterations, with the original buildings often claimed to have been destroyed by fire.

The stones are indeed crying out. Let's hear what they have to say, shall we?

Above: Hey, check it out, it's an amazing medieval castle or palace! No. It's merely the Connecticut State Capitol... in Hartford.

Above: It's a palace! It's a castle! It's a fort! No. It's merely Stadium High School, in Tacoma, Washington. Yeah, *a high school!*

A (Tall) Tale of Two Cities

To better highlight the apparent impossibility of constructing certain grand structures with the tools available during their respective periods, let's delve deeper into some specific examples from the "Dark Ages" and "Renaissance". Let us consider the technological challenges and limitations of the time.

Impossibility of Achieving Grand Structures with Period Tools

Chartres Cathedral (France)

- **Description:** Completed in 1220, Chartres Cathedral is a monumental example of Gothic architecture with its soaring spires, intricate stained glass windows, and vast expanse.

- **Impossibility:** The precision required for cutting and placing the massive limestone blocks, along with the intricate carvings, would have been impossible with the rudimentary tools of the time, such as simple chisels and hammers. The construction of flying buttresses to support the towering walls and large windows, essential for maintaining structural integrity, would have been beyond the capabilities of the period's technology.

Notre-Dame de Paris (France)

- **Description:** Built between 1163 and 1345, Notre-Dame features a complex Gothic design, including large rose windows and a vast vaulted ceiling.

- **Impossibility:** The construction of Notre-Dame's elaborate stone carvings and massive scale, utilizing only chisels, hammers, and wooden scaffolding, would have been virtually impossible. The precision required for ribbed vaults and pointed arches, necessary for the structural support of the cathedral, far exceeded the limitations of the construction techniques available at the time.

St. Peter's Basilica (Vatican City)

- **Description:** The current St. Peter's Basilica, completed in 1626, features Michelangelo's dome, the largest unreinforced concrete dome in the world.

- **Impossibility:** Constructing Michelangelo's dome with the technology of the early 17th century, which included rudimentary cranes and manual labor, was nearly impossible. The engineering required to support such a massive dome, alongside the precise control over concrete curing and placement, defies the capabilities of the tools and techniques of that era.

Palazzo Vecchio (Italy)

- **Description:** Constructed from 1299 onwards, the Palazzo Vecchio in Florence is renowned for its fortress-like appearance and colossal stone walls.

- **Impossibility:** The sheer scale of the Palazzo Vecchio's construction, including its massive stone walls, would have been impossible with the period's technology. The ability to cut, transport, and precisely align large stone blocks using only basic tools and manual labor is inconceivable.

The Doge's Palace (Italy)

- **Description:** Built between the 9th and 15th centuries, the Doge's Palace in Venice features intricate Gothic architecture and a detailed I.

- **Impossibility:** The detailed marble carvings and elaborate I of the Doge's Palace would have been impossible to achieve with the rudimentary stoneworking tools of the time. Additionally, the construction of a stable foundation in the lagoon bed using only period-appropriate methods would have been unfeasible.

El Escorial (Spain)

- **Description:** Constructed between 1563 and 1584, El Escorial is a massive royal monastery and palace known for its precise and orderly design.

- **Impossibility:** The scale and precision required for El Escorial's construction, including the intricate layout and massive size, would have been impossible to achieve with the technology available at the time. The transportation and placement of large materials, combined with the need for exact alignment, far surpassed the capabilities of period tools and methods.

The Basilica di Santa Maria del Fiore (Italy)

- **Description:** Also known as the Florence Cathedral, its construction began in 1296 and was completed with Brunelleschi's dome in 1436.

- **Impossibility:** The construction of Brunelleschi's dome, without external supports and utilizing advanced techniques, would have been impossible with the construction tools of the period. The precise engineering required for such a large dome, along with the sophisticated design, exceeded the capabilities of Renaissance-era technology.

The Tempietto (Italy)

- **Description:** Designed by Donato Bramante and completed in 1502, the Tempietto is celebrated for its classical proportions and Renaissance architecture.

- **Impossibility:** The construction of the Tempietto's perfectly symmetrical and detailed design would have been unachievable with the available tools. The precision required for the circular structure and the detailed decoration defies the technological limitations of the early 16th century.

The Uffizi Gallery (Italy)

- **Description:** Constructed between 1584 and 1593 in Florence, the Uffizi Gallery is known for its Renaissance architecture and role as a major art museum.

- **Impossibility:** The construction of the Uffizi Gallery's extensive and detailed I, along with its long corridors, would have been impossible using the tools and methods of the late 16th century. The scale and complexity of the building's design required advanced engineering capabilities beyond what was available at the time.

Mont Saint Michel (France)

- **Description:** Mont Saint Michel is a striking island commune located in Normandy, France. Its construction dates back to the 8th century, with the iconic abbey rising above the sea, built atop a rocky mount. Over the centuries, it evolved into a fortress, monastery, and pilgrimage site, attracting visitors from all over the world.

- **Impossibility**: The construction of Mont Saint Michel, particularly its Gothic abbey and towering spires, defies the engineering capabilities of the time. Built on a rocky island, surrounded by powerful tidal shifts, the building's complex design and structural stability would have been impossible without advanced technologies.

The monumental structures from the Dark Ages and Renaissance, such as Chartres Cathedral and St. Peter's Basilica, present an engineering and construction challenge that appears impossible given the tools and technology purportedly available at the time. The precision, scale, and complexity of these buildings suggest an advanced level of technological capability or alternative explanations beyond traditional historical understandings.

Creating a structure like the Milan Cathedral (above) would have been impossible with the tools available during the time of its supposed construction. According to historical accounts, it "took nearly six centuries to complete: construction began in 1386, and the final details were completed in 1965" (Wikipedia).

Mont Saint Michel, dedicated to the Archangel Michael, might well bear the mark of his handiwork. The sheer scale of the structure, coupled with the surrounding tides, would have posed insurmountable challenges for people reliant on the rudimentary tools and transportation available during that era.

The Giants of Old and the Architecture of the Ancients

The monumental architecture of the pre-modern world, particularly the vast cathedrals, colossal archways, and towering doorways, poses a tantalizing mystery: who were these grand structures designed to accommodate? Measurements alone are thought-provoking. The entrance to Notre Dame de Paris stands at an awe-inspiring height of 69 feet. The Arch of Constantine in Rome reaches 69 feet tall as well, while the Arc de Triomphe in Paris soars to 162 feet, with its central arch towering over 95 feet high. Why such enormous dimensions?

Could these structures have been built for a race of beings far taller than modern humans? Genesis 6:4 recounts the existence of *"giants in the earth in those days; and also after that,"* hinting at a world inhabited by extraordinary beings. Archeological finds—such as oversized human skeletons unearthed in America and other parts of the world—suggest that giants have indeed roamed the earth long after the antediluvian period.

Willis George Emerson's book *The Smoky God* describes a hidden civilization of giants living in the inner earth, based on Olaf Jansen's alleged journey to the North Pole. Could this lend credence to the phrase "giants *IN* the earth" from Genesis 6:4? If such beings were real, their size would make them the ideal builders of the towering cathedrals and arches scattered across the globe.

Another perspective considers the possibility of angelic involvement. Often described as towering in stature by eyewitnesses, could angels have constructed these edifices to reflect their own scale? Alternatively, some theories propose that these structures were erected during Christ's millennial reign to accommodate resurrected saints who ruled alongside Him—saints who may have been gifted with glorified bodies far larger than ordinary humans.

If these buildings were designed for a race of giants, who were these mysterious inhabitants? Were they survivors of the antediluvian world, angelic beings, or the resurrected saints given cities to rule over (see Luke 19:17)? Could their "founding" coincide with a historical "reset" in the late 1700s, an event that wiped clean the traces of their world and allowed a new narrative to emerge?

These colossal edifices, with their intricate designs and staggering dimensions, remain a testament to an enigmatic past that has been deliberately obscured. As we examine their scale, beauty, and craftsmanship, we are undoubtedly left asking: were they built for giants, and what does their existence reveal about the true history of our world?

Just one example of giant doors found on common cathedrals. There's probably one such giant doorway in a city near you.

Above: The "Arc the Triomphe" in Paris, France, despite its magnificent grandeur and apparent uniqueness, is just one of many giant archways found throughout the world. Other significant ones are the Arch of Titus and the Arch of Constantine in Rome, the Arch of Septimius Severus in the Roman Forum, the Arch of Hadrian in Athens, the Arch of Trajan in Benevento, and the Arch of Caracalla in Volubilis.

The Giant Stumps of the Past

"Thus were the visions of mine head in my bed; I saw, and behold a tree in the midst of the earth, and the height thereof was great. The tree grew, and was strong, and the height thereof reached unto heaven, and the sight thereof to the end of all the earth: The leaves thereof were fair, and the fruit thereof much, and in it was meat for all: the beasts of the field had shadow under it, and the fowls of the heaven dwelt in the boughs thereof, and all flesh was fed of it. I saw in the visions of my head upon my bed, and, behold, a watcher and an holy one came down from heaven; He cried aloud, and said thus, Hew down the tree, and cut off his branches, shake off his leaves, and scatter his fruit: let the beasts get away from under it, and the fowls from his branches: Nevertheless leave the stump of his roots in the earth [...]." ~Daniel 4:10-15a, KJV

The scriptures and apocryphal texts like Daniel (above) and 1 Enoch tell of giant trees that once reached to the heavens, providing sustenance and shelter for all living creatures. These trees, in an act of divine judgment, were hewn down by the command of God, carried out by angelic "watchers."

Could these accounts explain geological anomalies like Devil's Tower in Wyoming, which bears the unmistakable resemblance of a massive tree stump? The legend of Paul Bunyan and his fabled exploits may even echo a distorted memory of angelic missions to fell these immense trees that once symbolized the unbridled reach of a corrupted creation.

With other sites such as Mount Roraima in South America raising similar questions, could these formations be the final, silent witnesses of a world reshaped by divine decree, leaving only stumps as markers of an extraordinary past now hidden from our understanding?

Could these accounts explain geological anomalies like Devil's Tower in Wyoming, which bears the unmistakable resemblance of a massive tree stump? The legend of Paul Bunyan and his fabled exploits may even echo a distorted memory of angelic missions to fell these immense trees that once symbolized the unbridled reach of a corrupted creation.

With other sites such as Mount Roraima in South America raising similar questions, could these formations be the final, silent witnesses of a world reshaped by divine decree, leaving only stumps as markers of an extraordinary past now hidden from our understanding?

The Devil's Tower (ironic name) in Wyoming bears a striking resemblance to a giant tree stump. It was featured in the hit 70s movie: Close Encounters of the Third Kind.

Many strange rock formations found worldwide could very well be petrified tree stumps.

Mount Roraima in South America (Venezuela) also resembles a giant tree stump.

The Founding of Buildings and of Cities

As the Satanic Bloodlines, under the beneficial guise of Freemasons, Jesuits, Oddfellows, and other The Ruling Class secret groups, began their explorations in the early 19th century, they encountered abandoned cities, long forgotten and hidden by time, that bore witness to a lost era. These cities, characterized by magnificent, half-buried structures and vast, empty streets, were remnants of Christ's millennial reign. Many of these buildings were found to be intact, albeit buried or in disrepair, and their architecture far surpassed the capabilities of the time. Rather than these cities being newly constructed, the Freemasons stumbled upon them, recognizing an opportunity to claim them as their own and build their own worldwide empire of wealth and real-estate.

Observe the visible tops of windows at the very base of this downtown building in an old photograph. Could there be far more of this structure hidden underground?

Above: Could some of the antique buildings in the downtown areas of cities worldwide have been buried by a "mudflood"? Could there be more hidden beneath these structures than what we see on the surface?

What is often hidden from the historical record is that these cities were not "built" in the conventional sense by human hands in the 1700s or 1800s. Instead, they were "founded" (as historical sites, plaques, and texts attest) during this period. The difference in terminology is crucial. While "built" implies construction, the term "founded" (as in *found*) suggests that these structures were merely found—i.e. rediscovered and re-appropriated. The Freemasons did not build these cities—they found them, the remnants of an advanced and divine civilization, and took control of them. Furthermore, the term "Free Masonry" itself may allude to the idea of *free masonry*, implying that the Masons inherited or took over these cities and buildings without constructing them from scratch. They inherited "free buildings", a gift of sorts, from a forgotten past. And by claiming these architectural wonders as their own, they solidified their place as the new elite power—the new sheriffs in town.

This discrepancy between "built" and "founded" is often glossed over in historical narratives. For example, a building marked as having been "built in 1784" may have instead been merely reclaimed and refurbished by the Freemasons or other elites during this period. The original construction likely dates back to Christ's millennial reign, long before the supposed construction dates we see in history books. Many cities, including the grand structures of Paris, London, and across Europe and the Americas, were already in place—waiting to be rediscovered and claimed by those who were quick to rewrite history.

Moreover, this period of rediscovery was not without its spiritual implications. Following Satan's release from the pit, a secretive pact was made between influential elite families—such as the Rothschilds, Rockefellers, and many others—and Lucifer himself. This agreement granted these families unprecedented power over global resources, political systems, and the newly rediscovered cities. In return, Lucifer ensured their dominance over the world, which had been carefully manipulated to suit his Luciferian principles. This pact solidified their wealth and influence, allowing them to shape the emerging world order and erase the memory of Christ's millennial reign from the public's consciousness. These elites, aided by the Freemasons, then set out to reshape the historical narrative, presenting themselves as the creators and founders of the grand cities that once belonged to a divine kingdom.

By rewriting history and laying claim to these miraculous structures, they ensured that the remnants of Christ's reign would remain hidden in plain sight, repurposed to suit their own purposes. In this way, the Freemasons and elite families worked hand in hand with Lucifer, using the newly rediscovered cities and buildings of the millennial kingdom to cement their control over the world and obscure the truth of Christ's thousand-year rule.

The actual (and ominous) motto of the Oddfellows contains the words "Bury the Dead and Educate the Orphans." This phrase, seemingly charitable and compassionate, takes on a much more sinister implication when considered in the context of the events unfolding in the post-millennial world.

As the mudfloods, great fires, and other disasters ravaged cities and buried much of the population, countless children were left orphaned. The Oddfellows—and other secret societies tied to the Freemasons—stepped in to take control of these orphans. However, rather than merely caring for them, they used these children to repopulate the abandoned cities they had rediscovered and claimed. The immense loss of life required mass burials, while the influx of orphans provided the secret societies with a population they could mold, relocate, and control.

The phrase "Bury the Dead and Educate the Orphans" may also allude to the intentional silencing of survivors who had witnessed the millennial reign of Christ. Many of these individuals were committed to insane asylums, labeled as mad for their testimonies of a glorious past under Christ's rule. With witnesses either buried or institutionalized, the orphans became a clean slate, with no knowledge of their true heritage or the glorious cities they now occupied.

In essence, the motto of the Oddfellows served as both a mission statement and a cover for the elite's deeper, more deceptive plans: to bury the truth and reshape the future by controlling the youngest survivors of this newly rewritten world.

Above: The Oddfellows logo, dated 1834, represents one of the more enigmatic secret societies that thrived during the 1800s. The text of their modus operandi is quite revealing: *Visit the Sick, Relieve the Distressed, Bury the Dead, and Educate the Orphans.* Relieve the distressed—those left behind after the end of the Millennium and subsequent reset—by institutionalizing them in insane asylums. Bury the (many) dead, victims of the mudfloods, plagues, and the burning of cities. Educate—or rather brainwash and indoctrinate—the orphans with the new narrative, molding them into efficient worker bees for Satan's Little Season.

This historic photo of St-Petersburg, Russia taken in the 19th-century shows very few people found in the great square—at daytime, no less.

A view of the now-destroyed Tuileries Palace captured by Edouard-Denis Baldus around 1860. In the foreground, two men engage in conversation, while two small urchins crouch near the entrance to a fenced-off garden on the left. There are no other people visible in the scene.

A rare sight: Paris without people

Mysterious Star Forts

Star forts, also known as bastion forts or trace italienne forts, are a fascinating topic when exploring historical military architecture. They were designed in a distinctive star shape to enhance their defensive capabilities. Let's delve into their historical context, purpose, and the intriguing theories surrounding them.

Star forts emerged in the late 15th and early 16th centuries, primarily in Europe, during the Renaissance. Their design was a response to the advancements in artillery technology, which rendered traditional medieval castle designs ineffective against cannon fire. The star-shaped design, characterized by bastions and angular projections, is said by historians to maximize the field of fire and minimize blind spots, making them more resistant to sieges. But I suspect Star Forts are far more than meets the eye.

Examples of Star Forts

Several notable examples illustrate the grandeur and complexity of star forts:

- **Fort Saint-Elmo (Malta):** A key fortification during the Great Siege of Malta in 1565. Its design exemplifies the use of bastions to defend against a determined Ottoman assault.

- **Nossa Senhora da Graça Fort (Portugal):** Perched atop Monte da Graça near Elvas, Portugal, this 18th-century star fort is a marvel of military engineering. Built to guard the Portuguese-Spanish border, its intricate design and commanding position have fueled speculation about its possible ties to ancient star symbolism and esoteric traditions.

- **Fortress of Suomenlinna (Finland):** Built on a series of islands, this star fort is a testament to the strategic importance of controlling waterways and defending against naval threats.

- **Citadel of Vauban (France):** Named after the famous French military engineer Sébastien Le Prestre de Vauban, who revolutionized fortification design in the late 17th century.

- **Statue of Liberty Star Fort (USA):** The Statue of Liberty stands atop Fort Wood, an 11-pointed star fort built in the early 19th century as part of New York Harbor's coastal defenses. While officially designed for military purposes, the star-shaped structure has sparked theories linking it to occult symbolism and illuminist ideals, aligning with the statue's depiction as the "light-bringer."

Above: The Nossa Senhora da Graça Fort sits on top of Monte da Graça, near Elvas, Portugal.

Unbeknownst to most, the Statue of Liberty stands on its very own star fort-like structure.

The Great Fires of the 1800s and Early 1900s

Many of us who grew up attending summer camp recall singing "Mrs. O'Leary's Cow" around the campfire. The song, recounting the infamous legend of the cow sparking the Great Chicago Fire, was often presented as a communal chant. It embedded historical narratives into the memories of generations. Here are the lyrics:

Late last night, while we were all in bed

Old Lady Leary lit a lantern in the shed

And when the cow kicked it over

She shook her head and said:

It'll be a hot time in the old town tonight!

FIRE FIRE FIRE!

So, according to legend—Catherine O'Leary, a 35-year-old milk supplier, entered her barn carrying a lantern to see while milking her cow. The story claims that the cow kicked over the lantern, sparking a fire that ultimately consumed much of the city.

I believe having children repeatedly sing those lyrics around a campfire could be seen as a form of ritualistic indoctrination, subtly embedding the narrative of the event into their consciousness and normalizing the version of history being promoted at the time.

The great city fires of the 1800s and early 1900s were, in my opinion, orchestrated to erase physical evidence of Christ's

Millennial Kingdom. These catastrophic events, occurring in key cities worldwide and not just Chicago, resulted in the destruction of many buildings that could have been relics from an earlier, more advanced civilization—a time when Christ reigned and humanity prospered.

These fires are theorized to have conveniently "cleansed" certain cities of old-world architecture and artifacts, wiping out the grandeur that might have been evidence of Christ's millennial rule. Here's a list of some major fires during that time period:

1. The Great Fire of London (1834)

- **Date:** October 16, 1834
- **Location:** London, England
- **Description:** This fire destroyed much of the Palace of Westminster, including the House of Commons and House of Lords. The Gothic structures that were rebuilt in its aftermath, while grand, could have replaced even older, potentially millennial-era constructions.

2. The Great New York City Fire (1835)

- **Date:** December 16–17, 1835
- **Location:** New York City, USA
- **Description:** A devastating fire consumed much of Lower Manhattan, destroying hundreds of buildings in what was then the commercial heart of New York. Many buildings with historical architecture were lost,

possibly covering up remnants of millennial-era grandeur.

---

3. The Great Chicago Fire (1871)

- **Date:** October 8–10, 1871
- **Location:** Chicago, USA
- **Description:** This infamous fire destroyed approximately 3.3 square miles of Chicago, leaving a significant portion of the city in ruins. It is theorized that many old-world structures were intentionally destroyed, making room for modern architecture and erasing any trace of prior civilizations.

---

4. The Peshtigo Fire (1871)

- **Date:** October 8, 1871
- **Location:** Peshtigo, Wisconsin, USA
- **Description:** Occurring on the same day as the Great Chicago Fire, the Peshtigo Fire remains the deadliest fire in American history, killing an estimated 1,500–2,500 people. This fire consumed much of the surrounding area, and the synchronicity with the Chicago Fire raises questions about the purposeful destruction of millennial-era settlements.

---

5. The Boston Fire (1872)

- **Date:** November 9–10, 1872

- **Location:** Boston, Massachusetts, USA
- **Description:** This fire destroyed 65 acres of downtown Boston, including 776 buildings. Some believe that many ancient and intricately designed buildings were lost, potentially covering up remnants of a forgotten golden age.

6. The Great Fire of Moscow (1812)

- **Date:** September 14–18, 1812
- **Location:** Moscow, Russia
- **Description:** While much of Moscow was burned down during Napoleon's invasion, many structures were believed to have been from a much earlier era. This fire could have destroyed evidence of advanced millennial buildings, replacing them with post-Napoleonic reconstruction.

7. The Great Fire of Hamburg (1842)

- **Date:** May 5–8, 1842
- **Location:** Hamburg, Germany
- **Description:** This massive fire engulfed Hamburg, destroying much of the old city, including 1,700 residences and historical buildings. It was an opportunity for modernization, potentially eliminating architecture from a millennial period of Christ's reign.

8. The San Francisco Earthquake and Fire (1906)

- **Date:** April 18–21, 1906
- **Location:** San Francisco, California, USA
- **Description:** A massive earthquake followed by a devastating fire consumed much of San Francisco, burning thousands of buildings. This event is seen by theorists as possibly engineered to remove ancient structures hidden beneath layers of modern civilization.

9. The Great Seattle Fire (1889)

- **Date:** June 6, 1889
- **Location:** Seattle, Washington, USA
- **Description:** This fire consumed the entire central business district, leaving the city in ruins. Some argue that this cleared away remnants of Seattle's ancient architecture, making way for modern, industrial development.

10. The Great Baltimore Fire (1904)

- **Date:** February 7–8, 1904
- **Location:** Baltimore, Maryland, USA
- **Description:** This fire ravaged over 1,500 buildings in the heart of Baltimore. Many historical structures were destroyed, and with them, potentially priceless evidence of earlier advanced civilizations.

11. The Great Toronto Fire (1904)

- **Date:** April 19, 1904
- **Location:** Toronto, Ontario, Canada
- **Description:** This fire destroyed 122 buildings in Toronto's industrial center, wiping out many old-world architectural landmarks. Such destruction may have erased lingering traces of Christ's millennial kingdom from the New World.

12. The Great Yokohama Fire (1866)

- **Date:** November 26, 1866
- **Location:** Yokohama, Japan
- **Description:** The fire destroyed much of Yokohama, a key trading port. The rebuilding of the city may have covered up evidence of a previous advanced civilization present during Christ's reign.

13. The Great Constantinople Fire (1865)

- **Date:** September 1865
- **Location:** Constantinople (modern-day Istanbul), Turkey
- **Description:** This fire destroyed a significant portion of Constantinople, a city with ancient roots. Theories suggest that this fire may have eradicated ancient Christian architecture dating from the millennial reign of Christ.

14. The Great Vancouver Fire (1886)

- **Date:** June 13, 1886
- **Location:** Vancouver, British Columbia, Canada
- **Description:** A fire destroyed nearly all of Vancouver's buildings, laying waste to any ancient structures that could have revealed the truth about a forgotten era.

---

15. The Great Fire of Rome (1842)

- **Date:** September 1842
- **Location:** Rome, Italy
- **Description:** Rome, the eternal city, faced a significant fire in the mid-19th century. This blaze could have destroyed invaluable structures tied to Christ's rule, conveniently aligning with the push to obscure the true history of the millennial kingdom.

---

16. The Great Lyon Fire (1864)

- **Date:** September 12–13, 1864
- **Location:** Lyon, France
- **Description:** This fire swept through the heart of Lyon, obliterating buildings that had stood for centuries. Many believe that this was part of a wider agenda to erase evidence of Christ's millennial kingdom in Europe.

17. The Great St. John's'Fire (1892)

- **Date:** July 8, 1892
- **Location:** St. John's' Newfoundland, Canada
- **Description:** The largest fire in the history of St. John's wiped out the city center. Ancient structures of European origin were likely consumed, preventing future generations from understanding their true purpose and origin.

18. The Great Fire of Montreal (1852)

- **Date**: July 8, 1852
- **Location**: Montreal, Quebec, Canada
- **Description**: This fire destroyed over 1,100 buildings and displaced nearly 10,000 people, decimating much of the city's working-class area and altering Montreal's'urban development

19. The Great Fire of Toronto (1904)

- **Date**: April 19, 1904
- **Location**: Toronto, Ontario, Canada
- **Description**: Starting in a factory, this fire destroyed 104 buildings in Toronto's'downtown core. It caused significant financial losses but no fatalities, highlighting a turning point in urban fire prevention and safety measures

20. The Halifax Explosion (1917)

- **Date**: December 6, 1917
- **Location**: Halifax, Nova Scotia, Canada
- **Description**: A massive explosion occurred after a munitions ship collided with another vessel, leveling much of Halifax's north end, killing around 2,000 people, and leaving thousands injured or homeless

Erasing the Evidence of Christ's Reign?

From this perspective, these devastating fires of the 1800s and early 1900s spread across the world, seem far too coincidental. The fact that they targeted densely populated urban centers—each containing irreplaceable architecture that could have been remnants of a prior, more advanced civilization—is suspicious. Could these events have been orchestrated to wipe out physical evidence of a glorious millennial kingdom ruled by Christ?

These fires paved the way for modern architectural "advances," but they also conveniently erased much of the past. This pattern of destruction aligns with the broader theory that, upon his release from the pit, Satan sought to obscure the historical reality of Christ's earthly reign by erasing key artifacts, landmarks, and rewriting the narrative of world history.

Scarier yet is the fact that, in recent years, many "accidental forest fires" have set ablaze numerous places on the globe. Some have noted the probable use of DEW (Direct Energy Weapons) to ignite the fires and cause widespread destruction. Notable incidents include:

- **Canada Wildfires (March 2023–September 2023):** Beginning in March 2023, and with increased intensity starting in June, Canada was affected by a record-setting series of wildfires. All 13 provinces and territories were impacted, with large fires in Alberta, British Columbia, the Northwest Territories, Nova Scotia, Ontario, and Quebec. The 2023 wildfire season had the most area burned in Canada's recorded history, surpassing the 1989, 1995, and 2014 fire seasons, as well as in recorded North American history, surpassing the 2020 Western U.S. wildfire season.

- **Maui Wildfires (August 8, 2023):** Wind-driven fires devastated the island of Maui, particularly the historic district of Lahaina, resulting in over 100 fatalities and the destruction of more than 2,200 structures.

- **Los Angeles Wildfires (January 7, 2025):** Rapidly spreading fires in the Los Angeles area displaced upwards of 175,000 people and claimed at least five lives. The Palisades fire, the most destructive in Los Angeles County history, engulfed over 17,000 acres.

These incidents, and others all over the world, have led me to believe that perhaps another Great Reset is upon us. Let us hope and pray for a soon intervention of the God kind.

CHAPTER 6:

Historical Fabrications

"History is a set of lies agreed upon." ~Napoleon Bonaparte

"History is bunk." ~Henry Ford

One of the most intriguing aspects of the theory that Satan, upon his release from the pit, sought to obscure the memory of Christ's millennial reign is the possibility that hundreds of years were artificially added to our historical timeline. This addition would serve to create a narrative that distances humanity from the events of Christ's reign, pushing them further back in time, and thereby confusing and disconnecting people from their true history.

Were Centuries Added to the Historical Timeline?

Around 750–850 years, perhaps even more, were added to the historical record during the Middle Ages, which would explain why much of medieval history appears sparse, with long periods of little development or questionable accounts. These "phantom centuries" have been deliberately inserted to obscure the true timeline, pushing key events from Christ's millennial reign further into the distant past and into oblivion. By doing so, Satan and his allies could erase the memory of that divine era, making it nearly impossible for future generations to trace the truth about Christ's rule on Earth.

History, as we know it, may not be as linear or accurate as we've been led to believe. If Christ's return and millennial reign occurred on or around 70-73 AD, as scripture and historical clues suggest, and Satan was loosed from the pit on or around 1776, it raises a staggering question: How much of our timeline has been fabricated to obscure these monumental events?

By this calculation, roughly 800 years may have been added to our history, creating a false narrative that distances us from the truth of Christ's fulfilled promises and the prophetic timeline outlined in the Bible. This would mean we are not living in the year 2025, but rather closer to 1225-1325, a number that aligns far more closely with the unfolding of Satan's Little Season.

Of course, the implications, if accurate, are profound. These "added years" distort our understanding of technological progress, ancient architecture, and even the cultural shifts that have shaped humanity. This deception is not merely a historical curiosity—it is a deliberate effort to conceal the truth of Christ's reign and Satan's temporary dominion.

If we are indeed living in a manipulated timeline, it demands that we reevaluate everything we've been taught. More importantly, it calls us to discern the signs of the times with renewed vigilance.

The addition of fictional years to the historical timeline serves as a strategic tool for obscuring the reality of Christ's Millennial

Reign (73 AD–1073 AD) on Earth. This distortion aligns with Satan's role as the "father of lies" (John 8:44) and his mission to deceive the nations (Revelation 20:3). Here's how this deception functions:

Hiding the Fulfillment of Prophecy

• The Millennial Reign represents the fulfillment of Christ's victory over sin, death, and Satan. By obscuring its occurrence, Satan fosters doubt in biblical prophecy and redirects attention toward a future, speculative fulfillment. This leads many astray, even drawing them into New Age movements and philosophies that distort the gospel.

Trying to Change the Times and Laws

• By inserting fictional centuries into the historical narrative, Satan stretches humanity's perception of time, creating confusion about the timing of the Millennial Reign. This delays the urgency for repentance and faith, leaving many complacent in their spiritual lives.

Promoting Fake Narratives

• The extended timeline enables the proliferation of secular histories and false narratives (e.g., evolution, humanistic progress), which diminish Christ's reign and exalt human autonomy, leading to a distorted view of God's sovereignty and a reliance on human wisdom over divine truth.

Confusing Eschatology

• Through the manipulation of historical events, Satan creates confusion regarding the end times, encouraging false teachings that frame the Millennium as a purely future event, despite the fact that Christ Himself declared it would occur *in that generation* (Matthew 24:34).

Deceiving and Hijacking the Church

• This widespread deception weakens the Church by severing believers from their heritage of victory. Without acknowledging Christ's reign, the Church forfeits a significant portion of truth and loses much of its sense of purpose. This leaves Christians to believe a false narrative, attend a weekly social club based on half-truths, and place their hope in events that have already been fulfilled. Late revivalist Vance Havner was right when he said: *"The devil is not fighting religion. He's too smart for that. He is producing a counterfeit Christianity, so much like the real one that good Christians are afraid to speak out against it."*

The Merging of Historical and Biblical Context

The following quotes highlight the convergence between historical records and the apocalyptic descriptions found in the New Testament.

Josephus (1st Century AD):

On the destruction of Jerusalem in 70 AD, marking the close beginning of Christ's reign:

"There was a certain prophetic oracle, which was also written down, that Jerusalem would be taken, and the sanctuary burned, by right of war." (Jewish War, Book VI, Chapter 5).

This event aligns with the establishment of Christ's kingdom, where judgment began with Israel (1 Peter 4:17).

• *"Neither did any other city ever suffer such miseries, nor did any age ever breed a generation more fruitful in wickedness than this was, from the beginning of the world."* (The Jewish War, Book V, Chapter 10).

This mirrors Revelation 18:24, where the city is held accountable for the blood of prophets and saints, experiencing unparalleled judgment.

• *"It appears to me that the misfortunes of all men, from the beginning of the world, if they be compared to these of the Jews, are not so considerable as they were..."* (The Jewish War, Preface, Section 4).

This reflects the unparalleled tribulation described in Revelation 16:18, where a great earthquake signifies the magnitude of judgment.

• *"The famine widened its progress and devoured the people by whole houses and families... the dead bodies of the poor were thrown down from the walls into the valleys beneath."* (The Jewish War, Book V, Chapter 12).

This parallels the fourth horseman in Revelation 6:8, symbolizing death through famine and sword.

• *"It was God who condemned the whole nation and turned every course that was taken for their preservation to their destruction."* (The Jewish War, Book VI, Chapter 5).

This mirrors Revelation 18:8, where the "great city" (interpreted as Jerusalem) faces divine judgment and destruction.

• *"Now, there was then a great number of false prophets suborned by the tyrants to impose on the people, who denounced this to them, that they should wait for deliverance from God."* (The Jewish War, Book VI, Chapter 5).

This directly parallels Revelation 13:11-14 and Matthew 24:24, which speak of false prophets performing signs and wonders to deceive the masses.

Tacitus (1ˢᵗ Century AD):

• *"The East had long been teeming with rumors that men from Judea would rule the world."* (Histories, Book 5).

Tacitus acknowledges the belief that Christ's kingdom rose during this time.

• *"The greater part were firmly convinced that the ancient scriptures of the priests alluded to this very time when the East would triumph, and from Judea would go forth men destined to rule the world."* (Histories, Book 5).

Tacitus' acknowledgment of fulfilled prophecy mirrors Revelation's expectation of Christ's kingdom and judgment on Jerusalem.

• *"Prodigies had occurred, but their expiation was neglected, and men interpreted them rather as portents of impending doom."* (Histories, Book 5).

Tacitus refers to ominous / supernatural signs, similar to the apocalyptic imagery in Revelation 8:7-12, which describes cosmic disturbances and disasters.

• *"The Christians were convicted, not so much on the charge of arson as for the hatred of the human race... Mockery of every sort was added to their deaths."* (Annals, Book 15, Chapter 44).

This reflects Revelation 6:9-11, where the souls of the martyrs cry out for justice during the widespread persecution under Roman authorities.

• *"The gods, in their anger, gave the Romans the right to destroy Jerusalem, as it was an abominable city."* (Histories, Book 5).

Tacitus' view of divine judgment on Jerusalem corresponds with Revelation's depiction of God using foreign nations (Rome's role) to bring judgment (Revelation 17:16-17).

• *"The temple was destroyed, as if the gods themselves demanded an end to that impious city."* (Histories, Book 5).

This corresponds to Revelation 18:6-8, where the city is judged for its sins, particularly its rejection of God and persecution of the saints.

• *"Prodigies had occurred... in the sky appeared visions of armies in conflict, glowing temples, and the heavens themselves ablaze."* (Histories, Book 5).

This mirrors Revelation 6:13 and Matthew 24:30, describing celestial signs, perhaps even a sighting of the heavenly New Jerusalem, heralding divine judgment.

• *"The Jews, in their madness, rushed to their own destruction, as the gods deserted their sanctuary."* (Histories, Book 5).

This parallels Revelation 11:2, where the temple is given over to be trampled and destroyed.

• *"The city of Rome is drunk on the blood of nations, with her armies spreading terror far and wide."* (Histories).

Tacitus' description of Rome aligns with the beast (with Rome's role) in Revelation 13, wielding authority and bringing destruction.

Eusebius (4th Century AD):

On the spread of Christianity during the Millennial Reign (or "dark ages" as Satan prefers to call it):

• *"The doctrine of our Savior flourished mightily, spreading among all mankind."* (Ecclesiastical History, Book X).

These historical accounts converge with the prophecies of Revelation, showing that the events described in the Bible were not just future predictions but actual occurrences that shaped history, confirming the fulfillment of Christ's Millennial reign during the first century. Satan's addition of fictional years serves to sever this connection, preventing many from recognizing the victory that has already been won and the Kingdom that is already established.

Why Are the Writings of Josephus and Tacitus Relevant?

- **Both Josephus and Tacitus** are esteemed for their thorough and generally trustworthy records of first-century events. Their writings offer a valuable non-Christian perspective that aligns with biblical accounts and the fulfillment of prophecy.

- **Josephus**, a Jewish historian and priest under Roman sponsorship, provides an insider's account of Jewish culture and the Jewish War with Rome, offering crucial context for understanding biblical events. Josephus' description of the destruction of Jerusalem closely mirrors the prophecies of Jesus found in Matthew 24 and Luke 21.

- **Tacitus**, a Roman historian, had little interest in advancing Christianity and often expressed skepticism or disdain toward it. His references to early Christianity and Jesus serve as unexpected yet valuable corroboration. His documentation of Nero's persecution of Christians and the moral decay of Rome sheds light on the backdrop of warnings and judgments in the book of Revelation.

Main Connections to Revelation

Revelation 11:2 speaks of the holy city being trampled for 42 months, which aligns with the Roman siege of Jerusalem that lasted approximately 3.5 years. Josephus documents this exact timeline, offering historical context for this prophecy.

Revelation 18 describes the destruction of a great city, mourned by the nations. Both Josephus and Tacitus provide detailed accounts of the fall of Jerusalem, which was seen as a catastrophic event by the ancient world.

Revelation 19:11-21 speaks of Christ's judgment and victory. The writings of Tacitus and Josephus document how Jerusalem's downfall marked the fulfillment of divine judgment.

The writings of Josephus and Tacitus strongly suggest that much of Revelation's prophecy was fulfilled in the first century, particularly with the destruction of Jerusalem in 70 AD. This event, in conjunction with Christ's prophetic words, points to the current age as the "little season" of deception, as described in Revelation 20:7.

Were False Historical Figures Created?

Many believe that as an added measure to fill the gaps created by these phantom centuries, a variety of false historical figures were also invented and inserted into the timeline. These figures often serve as placeholders, filling in key roles in the narrative to make the history seem continuous and coherent.

Here's a list of some historical figures, believed by some to be either entirely fabricated or significantly mythologized, according to alternate and revisionist historical theories:

Dubious Religious Figures and Church Fathers

1. Saint Augustine
2. Saint Jerome
3. Origen of Alexandria
4. Tertullian
5. Eusebius of Caesarea
6. Saint Patrick
7. Saint Nicholas
8. Saint Christopher
9. Saint George

Dubious Monarchs and Rulers

10. Charlemagne
11. King Arthur

12. Alfred the Great
13. Ethelred the Unready
14. Harun al-Rashid
15. Pre-Norman English Kings
16. Early Scandinavian Kings
17. Merovingian Kings
18. Byzantine Emperors during the "Dark Ages"

Dubious Explorers

19. Christopher Columbus
20. Marco Polo
21. Leif Erikson

The possible creation (or mythologization) of these figures, and others, combined with the artificial addition of centuries to the timeline, helped to provide the necessary scaffolding for the false historical narrative that Satan and his allies sought to establish after his release from the pit. These figures served to distance humanity from the reality of Christ's reign and foster a sense of disconnection from the true spiritual and historical legacy of that period.

False Historical Figures or Hidden Identities?

Another interesting theory is that some historical figures of the past might have been cases of mistaken (or corrupted) identities.

Could it be that some of the greatest kings of history were, in fact, based on or inspired by the life of Jesus Christ? This idea is not as outlandish as it might initially sound. In the case of King Arthur, for example, the legendary monarch is often depicted with significant Christ-like qualities, such as his role as a savior of the people and his eventual prophesied return—

parallels that hint at a deeper connection to the Christian Messiah. Furthermore, Arthur's renowned "Round Table," composed of 12 knights, closely mirrors the 12 apostles of Christ. This alignment suggests that the story of King Arthur, whether myth or reality, could have been an allegory or symbolic retelling of Christ's life and teachings, adapted into a royal narrative during a time when Christianity was gaining prominence.

The iconography surrounding kings and Christ often reveals striking similarities. Christian art frequently portrays Christ as a regal figure, seated on a throne, adorned in royal robes, with a crown placed upon his head. This depiction has been mirrored in the imagery of monarchs throughout history, where kings and emperors are also shown in similar divine poses, often with symbolic crowns, scepters, and robes. The image of a king's coronation—an event marked by a ceremonial anointing—also has echoes in Christian rituals, particularly those linked to the concept of Christ as the "anointed one" (the Messiah). Furthermore, Christian iconography often emphasizes Christ's role as both a king and a shepherd, an archetype that could easily align with the symbolic functions of a ruler in medieval society. For example, the French kings were often depicted as "Christ's vice-regents" on Earth, reinforcing the notion of divine right and spiritual leadership.

This convergence of imagery could suggest that, in some instances, kings and legendary figures like King Arthur were intentionally portrayed with Christ-like qualities to imbue their reigns with divine authority, reinforcing the connection between religious and royal power. This blending of sacred and temporal authority can be seen as an effort to align kings with the figure of Christ, further embedding Christian values into the very fabric of governance during the Middle Ages and beyond.

Similarly, some theorists have proposed that King James I of England might have been more than just a monarch with a strong interest in scripture. They suggest that James was perhaps the Apostle James himself, resurrected to play a pivotal role in the Christian world's history. This theory stems from the idea that King James' commissioning of the King James Bible—a translation of unparalleled influence—was not merely a royal endeavor but an act of divine purpose, aligning with a spiritual mission that spanned the millennial reign of Christ. In this view, James could have been seen as a "millennium saint," immortalizing the word of God during a symbolic period of Christ's reign on Earth.

These theories hinge on the idea that key historical figures, especially those from the medieval period onward, might have had their identities hidden or obscured, reshaping them into Christ-like symbols or incarnations. Whether through the blending of religious myth and royal lineage or through historical revision, these ideas provoke a re-evaluation of how history may have been altered to fit spiritual and eschatological frameworks.

Arthur and his Knights of the Round Table experiences a vision of the Holy Grail, an illumination by Évrard d'Espinques (c. 1475). Could the Arthurian legend be based on the ruling of Christ and the apostles during the Millenium?

The Mystery of Ancient Coins and Altered Dates

Another compelling piece of evidence that supports the theory of an altered timeline comes from the study of ancient coins and inscriptions found on buildings. In many instances, dates that should correspond to the first millennium (i.e., after the birth of Christ) are inscribed with an "I" or "J" in place of the numeral 1. For example, instead of 1756, a coin or inscription might read I756.

The "I" on Ancient Coins and Buildings

Proponents of this theory argue that the "I" or "J" on these dates does not represent the number one, but rather stands for "Iesus" (Jesus) or "Ihēsous", indicating that the date was part of the reign of Christ. Thus, I756 would actually mean the 756th year of Christ's rule (Anno Domini, the year of the Lord), rather than 1756 in the modern sense.

This would mean that the current dating system has been altered to obscure Christ's millennial reign and artificially elongate the timeline. By replacing the "I" with a numeral 1, Satan's forces created the impression that these dates were part of the current era, further distorting historical perception.

Anno Domini

The Latin expression *Anno Domini* (A.D.), meaning "In the Year of Our Lord," is traditionally used to mark the years since the birth of Jesus Christ. However, this dating system, which has become the standard in much of the Western world, may not be as straightforward as it seems. It's plausible that the years marked as A.D. could have been altered, perhaps intentionally, to obscure or shift the true historical timeline, especially regarding the events of Christ's Millennial Reign.

One intriguing possibility is that the years attributed to the time of Christ's life and the subsequent centuries were counted during the Millennial Reign itself, which many believe occurred between the 1st and 2nd centuries. If, as some theories suggest,

Christ's return occurred around 70 A.D. and ushered in His reign, the years following that event could have been counted as the Millennial period—essentially marking the time of Christ's physical and spiritual dominion on earth.

In this context, when we look at ancient coins and their dates, we might find anomalies or discrepancies, such as the seemingly odd and deliberate alteration of dates—like "I745" instead of "1745." These irregularities could be part of an effort to either obscure the truth of the timeline or manipulate historical records to make it appear that a long period of history has passed when, in fact, much of it could have been hidden or erased during the span of the Millennium. The insertion of misleading dates might be part of a larger cover-up to disassociate the world from the reality of Christ's reign and the significance of the true historical period that unfolded during that time.

If the *Anno Domini* system is indeed tied to the years counted during Christ's Millennial reign, the "missing" years could represent the period of time when Satan was bound and society operated under divine rule. By altering or obscuring these dates, those in power may have been attempting to erase this significant spiritual chapter in history—one where Christ's reign brought peace and truth, but also one which posed a direct challenge to their control and influence. As such, the true dates may not reflect our current understanding of history, but rather reflect a reality intentionally hidden from the masses, leaving only fragments of evidence in the form of altered coins, documents, and records.

Evidence of Altered Dates on Buildings

In addition to coins, many historical buildings have similarly ambiguous inscriptions. In older cathedrals and structures across Europe, you can find dates like I500 or I800, which are now read as 1500 or 1800, but were likely originally intended to signify the number of years since Christ's reign.

Moreover, there are examples where these inscriptions appear to have been physically altered. The "I" in the date was often modified into a "1," erasing any evidence of its original significance. This subtle but effective change helped reinforce the false historical narrative that Christ's millennial reign had never occurred or was merely a distant, forgotten myth.

The Role of Freemasonry and The Ruling Class Manipulation

"And he shall speak great words against the most High, and shall wear out the saints of the most High, and think to change times and laws: and they shall be given into his hand until a time and times and the dividing of time." ~Daniel 7:25

This passage in Daniel speaks of the Antichrist's effort to alter times and laws, a theme that mirrors what has happened in history. The manipulation of dates and records is not mere coincidence but a deliberate action orchestrated by secret societies, including the Freemasons, aligned with Satan's agenda. These groups took control of cities once ruled under Christ's millennial reign, using their influence to suppress and rewrite history.

By altering dates on coins, buildings, and documents, these elites worked to obscure the truth of Christ's reign and replace it with their own dominion. The erasure of Christ's rule allowed these secret societies to establish themselves as the new rulers of the world, shaping the narrative to suit their purposes. Through their influence, the masses were detached from the divine truths of the past, making it easier for these elites to control the future.

The Antichrist's predicted act of changing times and laws has been underway for centuries, and the Freemasons' role in this deception continues today. It is a systematic effort to rewrite history and obscure the divine order once established. The manipulation of dates on coins and buildings was one of their many tactics. By obscuring the timeline and erasing the significance of Christ's rule, these elites could more easily manipulate the world into believing a false narrative. This allowed them to establish themselves as the new rulers of a world that had once belonged to Christ and His saints.

The Perfect Deception

The insertion of phantom centuries, the creation of false historical figures, and the alteration of dates on coins and buildings all form part of a larger, calculated plan to obscure the reality of Christ's millennial reign. These tactics, executed in concert by Satan and his allies after his release from the pit, have successfully deceived generations of people into believing in a fabricated historical timeline.

As this false history has become the accepted norm, Satan has ensured that humanity remains disconnected from its true spiritual past, blind to the evidence of Christ's rule on Earth. Instead, people are left adrift in a narrative shaped by lies, unable to see through the veil that has been carefully constructed around them.

CHAPTER 7

Technology During the Millenium

*"If you want to find the secrets of the universe,
think in terms of energy, frequency, and vibration."* ~Nikola
Tesla

During the Millennial Reign of Christ, as described in Revelation 20:1-6, the world is often envisioned as being restored to a state of divine order, harmony, and glory. Proponents of speculative theology suggest that cymatics, or the study of how sound frequencies affect physical matter, may have played a profound role during this time, aligning creation with divine intention through vibrational energy.

Cymatics demonstrates how sound vibrations organize matter into complex patterns. When sound waves pass through mediums like water, sand, or air, they create stunning geometric designs that often resemble natural structures. This concept reveals how sound can shape and harmonize matter, hinting at the deeper connection between divine intention, frequency, and creation.

Cymatics in a Restored Creation

1. **The Divine Word and Cymatic Energy.** In biblical theology, God's Word is seen as the ultimate creative force. Genesis 1 describes how God spoke creation into existence, and John 1:1-3 identifies Christ as the "Word" through whom all things were made. Cymatics reflects this truth by showing that sound has the power to organize and create structure. During the Millennial Reign, Christ's direct rule could have restored creation to a state where divine frequencies—emanating from His Word—reordered the world into perfect harmony.

2. **Healing Frequencies and Vibrational Energy.** Sound waves may have been utilized to heal physical bodies and the earth itself. Isaiah 35:5-6 describes a time of miraculous restoration: the blind will see, the deaf will hear, and the lame will leap like a deer. If cymatic energy was harnessed, it could have facilitated these miracles, resonating at frequencies that restored broken bodies and ecosystems to their intended glory.

3. **Resonant Architecture.** Structures built during the Millennial Reign might have incorporated cymatic principles. Star forts, domes, and cathedrals—often noted for their perfect acoustics and geometric beauty—could have been designed to resonate with divine frequencies. These buildings would not only serve as places of worship but also amplify harmonic energy, fostering peace, healing, and unity among those who dwelled within them.

4. **Harmonization of Creation.** The animal kingdom, agriculture, and even weather systems may have been subject to divine vibrational order. Isaiah 11:6-9 depicts a world where the wolf lives with the lamb, and the earth

is filled with the knowledge of the Lord. Cymatic principles could explain how divine energy permeated the natural world, aligning every element with Christ's peaceable kingdom.

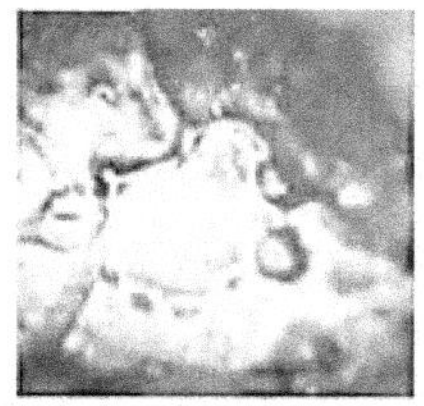

Water Molecule,
Before Offering a Prayer

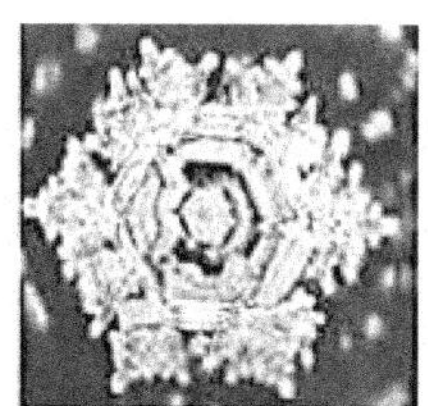

Water Molecule,
After Offering a Prayer

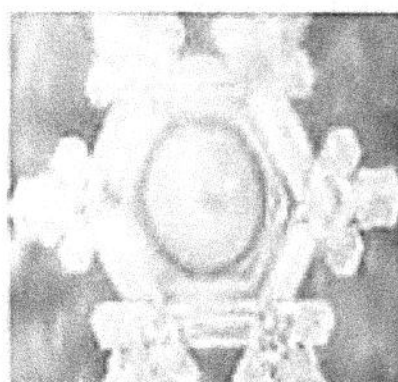

Thank You

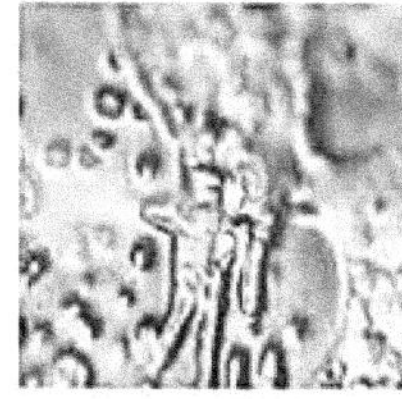

You Make Me Sick,
I Will Kill You

Love and Appreciation

Consider the effect that spoken words (vibrations) have on these water molecules. Still think your words are powerless? Now imagine the Word of God.

Cymatics and the Great Deception

Following the Millennial Reign, as Satan is released for his "little season" (Revelation 20:7-9), the knowledge and use of cymatics may have been corrupted or suppressed. What was once a divine tool for harmony could have been hidden, replaced by the chaos of human ambition and Satanic manipulation. The destruction of advanced cymatics technology, such as star forts, and its replacement with mundane, industrial constructs, fits within the narrative of Satan's effort to erase the memory of Christ's rule—or simply his incapacity to reproduce it or use it.

Cymatics offers a glimpse into how sound and frequency could have been employed during Christ's Millennial Reign to bring harmony, healing, and divine order to creation. As we examine its principles, the beauty and interconnectedness of God's design become evident. However, during Satan's Little Season, the loss or perversion of this knowledge underscores humanity's descent into chaos and deception, reinforcing the cyclical battle between divine truth and worldly manipulation.

The millennial reign of Christ, as described in alternative interpretations of history, was a time of extraordinary advancement not only spiritually but also in terms of harnessing natural energy. It is believed that the people of that era, under Christ's divine leadership, developed an advanced understanding of energy by tapping into the natural elements of water and vibration, creating a harmonious and efficient system for powering cities, buildings, and entire communities. Evidence of this sophisticated knowledge can still be seen in the remnants of star forts, cathedrals, and other monumental structures found around the world.

The Missing Elements

The periodic table of the elements, as we know it today, is a product of 19th-century scientific formalization. It contains 118 elements. However, there are whispers of an earlier, more complete table—one that included 18 "lost elements," foundational to the advanced technologies of the millennial reign of Christ. Chief among these is *aether* (pronounced "ether"), a substance once thought to permeate the universe, enabling free energy and instantaneous communication.

Aether: The Key to Lost Technology?

The concept of aether was central to pre-modern science, viewed as the medium through which light and energy traveled. Inventors like Nikola Tesla tapped into this understanding, theorizing that aether could provide limitless, sustainable energy. Tesla's work on wireless energy transmission and his designs for energy towers like the Wardenclyffe Tower suggest he rediscovered remnants of this divine technology. If harnessed, this energy source could have eliminated humanity's dependence on fossil fuels and decentralized power—making enslavement through economic systems nearly impossible.

The Tesla Broadcast Tower, 1904—aka Wardenclyffe Tower.

What Happened to the Lost Elements?

The absence of these elements raises two possibilities:

1. **Deliberate Suppression by Satan's Agents:** After Satan's release from the abyss (Revelation 20:7-8), the ruling elites of his "little season" may have worked systematically to suppress this knowledge. The removal

of aether from scientific discourse could have been a strategic move to keep humanity enslaved, forcing reliance on controlled, inefficient energy systems. By hiding or discrediting the science behind aether, Satan ensured his dominion remained unchallenged.

2. **Divine Protection of Sacred Knowledge:** Alternatively, God may have rendered this knowledge inaccessible to Satan after his release. If aether and the other lost elements were pivotal to the reign of Christ and His saints, their removal could have been an act of divine sovereignty, ensuring Satan could not wield or corrupt these tools for his purposes.

While there is no concrete list of these elements, historical and esoteric texts reference substances like *phlogiston, orichalcum, electrum,* and other mystical materials associated with pre-modern science and ancient civilizations. Aether remains the centerpiece of this mystery, but other lost elements may have been key to the construction of grand cathedrals, star forts, and advanced healing technologies.

Implications for Satan's Little Season

The removal of these elements and the suppression of their associated technologies have profound implications:

- **Technological Regression:** Humanity's inability to access free energy has fostered reliance on exploitable systems, enabling Satan's agents to maintain control.
- **Erasure of History:** The lost elements might have been instrumental in maintaining the infrastructure and prosperity of Christ's millennial reign. Their absence ensures that the glory of that era is relegated to myth or obscured entirely.

- **Aether's Revival in Modern Thought:** Aether's reemergence in Tesla's work may indicate that remnants of this divine knowledge are resurfacing. However, the suppression of Tesla's inventions shows that Satan's influence remains strong, quashing any technology that could liberate humanity.

The story of the lost elements is not just about forgotten science; it's about the war over humanity's knowledge and freedom during Satan's little season. Whether suppressed by Satan or protected by God, the absence of these elements reminds us of the unprecedented advancements and divine order of the millennial reign—a past deliberately obscured to maintain humanity's spiritual and material enslavement.

Star Forts as Energy Sources

Star forts, with their precise geometric designs and strategic locations, were not simply military structures, as often claimed in modern history. These forts, typically located near bodies of water or where rivers converge, may have served a more significant purpose in the millennial reign: as centers of energy production and distribution. The intricate star-shaped design, combined with their proximity to water, suggests that these citadels could have been harnessing the flow of water to generate power.

Water, a key conductor of energy, would have been channeled through the star fort's moats, trenches, and internal waterways, using the natural movement of currents to generate power in a way we no longer fully understand. The star-shaped design, with its multiple points and angles, may have amplified the natural flow of energy, capturing the water's kinetic force and converting it into usable power for the surrounding city. This theory posits that the star forts were not just fortresses but integral parts of a larger energy grid, tapping into Earth's natural resources in a way that aligns with the divine order of the millennial era.

Cathedrals and the Power of Vibration

Cathedrals, with their towering spires and massive domes, are some of the most impressive structures from the old world. However, their grandeur goes beyond religious or architectural significance. It is theorized that these buildings were designed to harness the power of vibrations, creating energy through resonance and frequency.

The large domes and high ceilings of cathedrals act as resonance chambers, amplifying sound waves and vibrations. Vibrational energy, generated through the very structure of the building, could have been used to create and distribute power. The cross-shaped design of many cathedrals, aligned with sacred geometry, would have enhanced this effect, allowing the cathedral to serve as a massive harmonic energy conductor. When choirs sang hymns or bells rang in these sacred spaces, the sound waves may have interacted with the architecture to create vibrational frequencies capable of generating energy.

The use of water in conjunction with sound could have further augmented this energy production. Many cathedrals were built near rivers or bodies of water, with aqueducts and water channels often hidden beneath the structures. Water, being an excellent conductor of energy, may have worked in tandem with the vibrations, creating a dynamic energy grid that powered the surrounding communities.

Above: Cathedral domes, such as this magnificent one,
may have been constructed for much more than grandiosity and aesthetics.

Above: A side-by-side comparison of cathedral windows compared to cymatic sound frequencies.

For Whom the Bell Tolls

In the context of the *millennial reign* and the potential spiritual and physical effects of the large bells in cathedrals, their role could be interpreted as being tied to the divine authority and protection established during this period. According to biblical prophecy, particularly in the book of Revelation (20:1-6), the thousand-year reign of Christ brings peace and restoration, where Satan is bound and the faithful reign with Christ. This period is envisioned as one where divine order is firmly established, bringing both spiritual and physical healing to the earth.

Given the theory that cymatics and vibrational energy played a role in this time of spiritual harmony, it is plausible to consider that the resonant frequencies of large bells were used to amplify this divine order. As noted in historical and theoretical studies, bells are believed to affect the environment through their sound waves, potentially aligning with the concept of "holy vibrations" that could have had a profound effect on people and the land during the millennial reign. The concept of sound frequencies creating harmony and alignment with divine purposes during the reign of Christ could reflect this idea.

Healing and Protection Through Resonance: During the millennial reign, the sound of bells could have served not only to signify sacred time and space but also to resonate in harmony with the divine order Christ brings. Just as cymatics and vibrational energy have been theorized to heal the body and spirit, the bell's deep tones may have been seen as a way to maintain peace and health. Their frequencies could have been thought to purge negativity and promote divine peace, reinforcing the idea that Satan's influence was restrained and divine authority prevailed. This ties into a larger cosmological theory that physical and spiritual realms are aligned during the millennial reign, offering a period of sanctification and spiritual restoration.

Furthermore, the deep tones of these bells, capable of reaching vast distances, would serve as a symbolic reminder that Christ's reign reaches beyond just the earthly realm—extending into the heavens, protecting the faithful, and maintaining cosmic balance during this time of unprecedented peace. The bells, resonating with harmonic frequencies, could then have been part of a divine system of protection against evil forces, unclean spirits and demons, including any residual spiritual forces that might have lingered from the previous, more tumultuous ages.

The widespread removal of church bells across Europe during World War II may have had far darker intentions than simply melting them down for artillery production. Their spiritual and physical healing properties were thus made impotent.

Organs Healing Organs

One of the most awe-inspiring features of grand cathedrals is the pipe organ, an instrument of unmatched scale and power. Historically, the massive organs within these sacred spaces were not merely for musical accompaniment but were potentially instruments of vibrational healing, tuned to resonate with both the architecture and the human body.

Resonance and Healing Through Sound

- **Harmonic Frequencies:** The tones produced by cathedral organs were often meticulously tuned to create resonances within the cathedral's vaulted ceilings and stone walls. These resonances may have amplified specific frequencies known to harmonize with the human body, promoting healing and equilibrium. Sound waves, particularly at certain frequencies, are theorized to stimulate the body's cells and even repair damaged tissues.
- **Architectural Symbiosis:** Cathedrals were designed with precision to amplify the organ's sound, channeling its vibrations throughout the structure. This synergy of sound and space could envelop worshippers in frequencies that restored their mental and physical well-being.

Healing Through Sacred Vibration

- **The Vibrational Spectrum:** Ancient traditions have long associated specific tones with healing properties. The organ, with its ability to produce a full spectrum of frequencies, could act as a therapeutic tool, addressing ailments ranging from stress to chronic pain.

- **Heart and Soul Alignment:** The deep, resonant bass notes might have affected the body's core, aligning internal rhythms such as heartbeats, while higher notes could have sharpened mental clarity and spiritual awareness.

A Divine Technology Lost?

With the rise of Satan's little season, the full potential of these instruments as tools of healing may have been intentionally forgotten or suppressed. Just as other divine technologies from the millennial reign were obscured, the therapeutic applications of sound were reduced to mere musicality. The immense pipe organs became relics of the past, stripped of their original purpose as conduits for both worship and wellness.

Connection to Vibrational Medicine

Modern science is rediscovering the power of sound in fields like vibrational medicine and cymatics, where frequencies are used to heal ailments and even break apart diseased tissues. This contemporary research echoes the potential use of cathedral organs as early, God-inspired instruments of healing. Could it be that the ruling elites, under Satan's influence, sought to remove this ancient wisdom to further enslave humanity to pharmaceutical dependency?

The power of cathedral organs wasn't just in their ability to fill spaces with glorious sound but in their potential to heal, rejuvenate, and elevate the human spirit. Stripped of this knowledge, we are left with fragments of their purpose, wondering at the divine ingenuity that was silenced during Satan's brief reign.

Water, Vibration, and Energy Creation

The relationship between water, vibration, and energy seems to have been a fundamental principle of the millennial reign. Most of the great cathedrals and monumental structures from this era are found near rivers, lakes, or coastlines, which is no coincidence. Water was not only a means of transport or sustenance but an essential element in creating energy.

Flowing water, channeled beneath these massive structures, would have interacted with the natural vibrations of the Earth and the resonance of the buildings themselves to generate power. Some theorists believe that this knowledge was part of divine wisdom, imparted during Christ's reign to create an abundant, clean, and harmonious energy system.

The star forts may have served as nexus points in this system, distributing energy across vast distances. Meanwhile, cathedrals and other sacred structures could have acted as local energy hubs, drawing power from both water and sound to sustain the spiritual and physical needs of the population.

Cymatics in the Millennium

The concept of cymatics— the study of the visible patterns created when sound frequencies interact with a medium like water— is explored as a potential facet of the technologies and spiritual principles operative during Christ's millennial reign. This theory proposes that ancient civilizations, particularly during this period, had access to advanced technologies, which included the ability to harness sound frequencies in a way that impacted both the physical and spiritual realms. The connection between water, sound, and vibration may have been understood and utilized to promote healing, balance, and spiritual enlightenment during this time.

Cymatics, as explored by Masaru Emoto, revealed that water can respond to sound waves in ways that alter its molecular structure. His research shows that music, words, and even thoughts can affect the crystalline formation of water, suggesting that sound frequencies could influence the body's energetic and cellular state. The therapeutic potential of water, when exposed to these vibrations, can be understood as a form of divine technology that might have been prevalent during the Millennium. This connection hints at the idea that Christ's reign could have included the widespread use of these sound-water technologies for physical healing, emotional restoration, and spiritual alignment.

Solfeggio frequencies—particular tones associated with ancient sacred music—are often referenced in connection with cymatics. These frequencies are believed to resonate with the natural harmonic vibrations of the body, facilitating healing and balance. During Christ's millennial reign, this sacred knowledge might have been fully realized and integrated into everyday life, enabling people to heal through divine frequencies that tuned both body and spirit to a higher plane of existence. Sound healing, used alongside water vibration therapy, would have created an environment where individuals could experience both physical restoration and spiritual ascension.

As we consider these theories, we can speculate that the "Millennium technology" used in Christ's time went beyond spiritual practices and extended into physical realities, facilitating healing and harmony through vibration and sound. This divine technology, once readily available, may have been suppressed or forgotten in later eras, leaving us only with fragmented knowledge of its potential. In *Satan's Little Season*, it is posited that these ancient practices, once central to Christ's reign, could hold keys to understanding both the hidden history of the past and the possibilities of the future. Through the lens of cymatics, sound frequencies, and their spiritual implications, we see that the connection between Christ's reign and divine technologies might have been far more profound than traditionally acknowledged.

CHAPTER 8:

Suffer the Little Children

"But whoever causes one of these little ones who believe in me to stumble, it would be better for him if a huge millstone were hung around his neck and that he were sunk in the depths of the sea." ~Jesus Christ, Matthew 18:6, World English Bible (WEB)

The manipulation and commodification of children are not merely modern phenomena; they are, unfortunately, deeply rooted in the fabric of society, with sinister threads woven throughout history. Today's child trafficking rings are nothing new; they are merely the latest manifestation of an age-old scheme to control and exploit the most vulnerable among us. From the grand spectacles of the World's Fairs in the late 19th and early 20th centuries, where "incubator babies" were paraded as technological marvels, to the chilling reality of orphan trains relocating children to abandoned cities, we see a pattern of dehumanization that echoes through the ages.

In the 1800s and early 1900s, child labor was rampant, with countless children subjected to grueling work in factories, mines, and fields, stripped of their innocence in exchange for profit. These children were often treated as mere cogs in a machine, reinforcing the idea that their lives were expendable commodities. This exploitation parallels today's trafficking networks, which continue to prey on children, using them for labor, sexual exploitation, and as tools in a larger Luciferian game of societal control.

The overflowing orphanages of the past raise unsettling questions. Why were so many children abandoned? Could it be that their parents were confined en masse to notorious insane asylums like the Willard Asylum in New York or the Toronto Asylum in Canada, where thousands were housed and forgotten? This grim reality suggests a concerted effort to erase the communal knowledge of the past and the nuclear family structure, leaving children vulnerable to being molded and indoctrinated into a new historical narrative under The Ruling Class who partnered with Satan upon his release.

Orphanages themselves became indoctrination centers, carefully designed to brainwash the next generation into accepting the prevailing social order. Instead of nurturing the innate potential of these children, these institutions often prioritized conformity over individuality, stripping away their identities in favor of a collective ideology—a strategy still used to this day. With each passing generation, the narrative has shifted, leaving us to question who truly benefits from the systematic exploitation and control of our youth.

In unraveling these threads, we see a chilling conspiracy at play—one that stretches across time and space, aimed at subjugating the innocent. The enemy knows that by targeting children, he can not only manipulate individual lives but also reshape the very foundations of society, and own the future.

The stakes are alarmingly high, and as we connect these dots, we are compelled to confront the darker truths lurking beneath the surface of our collective history.

Infant Incubators of the Late 1800's and Early 1900's

In the late 19th and early 20th centuries, infant incubators were hailed as symbols of scientific progress, celebrated for their ability to save premature infants. Yet beneath the veneer of medical advancement lies a shadowy and unsettling narrative. These so-called "child hatcheries," spearheaded by the enigmatic Dr. Martin Couney, were exhibited not in hospitals but at world fairs, expositions, and even Coney Island's carnival-like boardwalk from the 1890s through the 1930s. While Couney claimed to have saved thousands of lives through his incubators, questions about their true purpose—and the man behind them—cast a sinister pall over their history.

Dr. Couney, whose credentials remain murky at best, claimed to have trained under prominent French obstetrician Pierre-Constant Budin, yet no official documentation supports this assertion. Despite—or perhaps because of—his mysterious background, Couney presented his incubators not as mere medical devices but as spectacles for public consumption. For the price of admission, curious onlookers could gawk at rows of glass enclosures housing premature infants. He described the devices as "child hatcheries," " term both intriguing and disturbing in its implications.

While ostensibly altruistic, the context and sheer scale of Couney's exhibitions have raised unsettling questions. The large numbers of premature infants displayed, coupled with the lack of hospital records documenting their origins, has led some to speculate whether these incubators were used for purposes beyond neonatal care. Could they have been experimental growth chambers, devices designed to incubate more than just premature babies? This theory gains traction when considering the simultaneous surge in "orphan trains" during the same period—a movement that saw thousands of orphaned children transported across the United States to repopulate cities and towns in the rapidly expanding West.

The orphan train phenomenon raises troubling questions about the inexplicable ratio of orphaned children during this era. Where did all these children come from, and why was there such an urgent need to relocate them? Could the infant incubators have been part of a larger, more nefarious agenda to produce and grow children en masse? The eerie alignment of these events—the public spectacle of the incubators, the mysterious surge of orphaned children, and the industrialization of family structures—suggests a chilling possibility that remains largely unexplored.

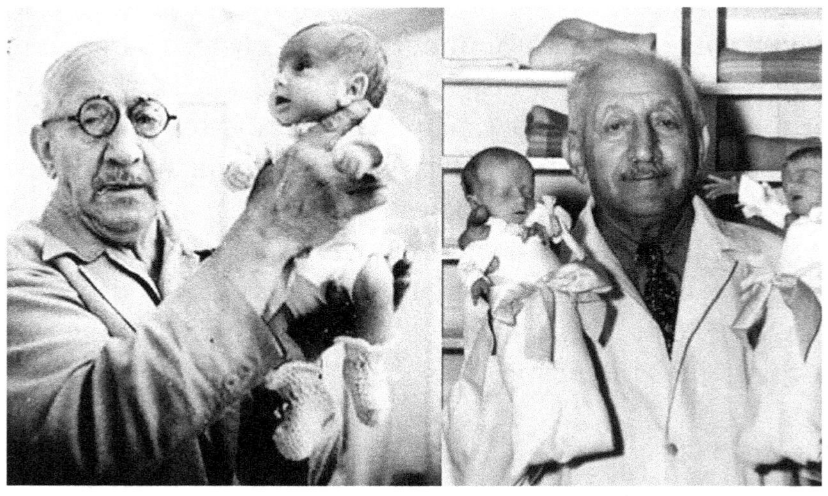

"Doctor" Martin Couney, holding up infants from his infant incubators.

The Real Cabbage Patch Kids

One aspect of post-millennium or post-reset theories involves the movement of orphaned children during the late 1800s and early 1900s.

During this period, hundreds of thousands of orphaned children were transported across America, often by train or even through the postal service, from the Eastern to the Western states. According to the mainstream narrative (i.e. fabricated lies), this was done to improve the lives of these orphans and to address a shortage of farm laborers in the West.

Adding to the mystery, many World's Fairs featured "Incubator Baby" exhibits. Signs at these exhibits announced "Living Babies," and rows of supposedly premature infants were displayed in showcases as the main attraction. Visitors could view them for a fee, often just a dollar. The sheer number of premature babies exhibited at these fairs raises questions.

The strangeness deepens further when we consider the French postcards of the time. Hundreds of postcards featured surreal, early photoshopped images depicting babies and toddlers being "born" from cabbages. This motif wasn't limited to static images—one of the earliest and most enigmatic films ever created, *La Fée aux Choux* (*The Cabbage Patch Fairy*), depicted this very idea and was premiered at one of the World's Fairs. It's also speculated that this imagery inspired the creation of the Cabbage Patch Kids later on.

There's a curious linguistic connection as well: could the term "choo choo train" actually derive from "chou chou train"? In French, *chou chou* was a term of endearment for small children during that era. Some postcards even depicted children, trains, and cabbages together, adding yet another layer to the mystery.

While the official accounts suggest benevolence, skeptics have questioned whether these events had a darker purpose. Some speculate these orphans may have been relocated after a significant war, possibly as a method of resettlement or even repopulation. Others suggest cloning might have been involved.

The presence of incubator babies further complicates the story. These infants were allegedly premature newborns from impoverished mothers in the surrounding areas. However, the sheer volume of these displays at multiple fairs is puzzling. Some theorists argue that the World's Fairs might have served as re-education centers following a great societal reset. Documents have surfaced indicating that teenage girls were taught child-rearing skills at these fairs—an unexpected focus for such grand public events. Were these teenage girls themselves older reset orphans being retrained for a new societal role?

Theories abound, and the timeline of events aligns with a broader reset around 1850. Some suggest this period followed a major conflict misrepresented in history, such as the so-called War of 1812. Interestingly, both Washington, D.C., and Moscow experienced significant fires in 1812, allegedly during separate wars. Could these events have been interconnected in a larger conflict or cataclysm unspoken in history books?

While much remains uncertain, the peculiarities surrounding orphan trains, incubator babies, and cabbage patch babies suggest a reality far more intricate than what official history conveys. One researcher speculated that cabbage patch babies might have been part of God's method for enacting the second resurrection—the "rest of the dead"—to repopulate the earth following the post-millennial vacancy. According to this unconventional theory, God may have used cabbage patches to supernaturally bring forth literal babies, who were subsequently found and sold to families through marketing postcards.

Though such ideas seem far-fetched, at this point, little would be surprising. After all, as John the Baptist declared:

*"And think not to say within yourselves, We have Abraham to our father: for I say unto you, that God is able of these stones to raise up children unto Abraham." ~*Matthew 3:9

A picture from the very strange 1896 French movie, one of the earliest ones ever made, "La Fée aux Choux"

Above: just one postcard (of many) from the late 1800s that depicted high strangeness: babies born from cabbages—the original cabbage patch kids. The text from this bizarre cabbage patch postcard reads: "There are those who smile, others who shed tears. There are those who coo, and others who are afraid."

Orphanages: Indoctrination Centers for the Next Generation

Orphanages throughout history, particularly in the 19th and early 20th centuries, have often been portrayed as sanctuaries for abandoned or orphaned children. However, in the context of *Satan's Little Season*, these institutions take on a more insidious role as potential indoctrination centers, designed to mold the next generation according to the prevailing political and religious ideologies of the time.

The massive structures used as orphanages during the 1800s and early 1900s often carried a sense of eerie grandeur, which, in hindsight, seems to contrast starkly with the grim purpose they served. These towering, castle-like buildings were typically designed to house large numbers of orphans, yet their imposing architecture often had a cold, institutional feel that could be seen as a reflection of the times' harsh attitudes toward the vulnerable. Far from being purely benevolent, many orphanages were, in reality, controlled environments that sought to reshape the identity of children, often separating them from their native cultures, values, and family structures. In the process, they were raised to be compliant citizens, taught to accept authority without question, and inculcated with the values that supported the broader agendas of those in power. This aligns with the idea that during times of social and political upheaval, children—regarded as the future of the state— became primary targets for reprogramming through controlled environments like orphanages, ensuring they would grow up in alignment with a new world order.

The architectural style itself—massive, sometimes almost monolithic in nature—seemed to echo a deep-seated societal need for control and order, echoing the institutionalized nature of social welfare at the time. It's worth considering whether these large, intimidating structures may have been built as more than mere practical buildings, but as a way to project authority, discipline, and obedience, while also serving as a reminder of the unseen structures that governed society's most vulnerable. In the context of the times, these orphanages became a haunting symbol of neglect, abandonment, and a more sinister and hidden agenda. It's no wonder that many of them were torn down.

Here are a few examples that fit the description of large, somewhat eerie institutions:

1. **The Industrial School for Boys (Nova Scotia, Canada):** "Founded" in the late 19th century, the Industrial School for Boys in Nova Scotia was designed to house orphans and children from poor families. The imposing structure was meant to serve as both a shelter and a place for the boys to learn practical trades. However, the school's strict discipline and forced labor policies, combined with its remote location, have led to accusations of harsh treatment, abuse, and isolation. Its architectural grandeur was built on the backs of the labor and suffering of these children.

2. **The St. Joseph's Orphanage (Cleveland, Ohio, USA):** Hailing from the late 1800s, St. Joseph's Orphanage was a large institution with a massive Gothic-style building designed to accommodate hundreds of children. While the orphanage had the outward appearance of a place of care and refuge, it was also the site of widespread physical and emotional abuse. The children were housed in cramped, overcrowded conditions, and many were subjected to neglect and mistreatment. The building's towering,

monolithic appearance contrasted with the often grim and disturbing conditions inside.

3. **The Orphanage of St. Vincent de Paul (Paris, France):** "Founded" in the early 19th century, this orphanage was one of many large institutions constructed in France during that time. It became infamous for its strict and sometimes harsh regime, and its grand architecture was seen as a reflection of the institutionalized view of orphans as a societal burden to be contained and controlled. Despite its beautiful and grand exterior, the orphanage operated in a manner that often led to neglect and abuse of the children under its care.

4. **The Foundling Hospital (London, UK):** "Established" in 1739, the Foundling Hospital in London was one of the first charitable institutions dedicated to caring for abandoned children. Its towering building, designed by prominent architects, was meant to serve as both a refuge and a symbol of social control. Over time, the Foundling Hospital became a large, sprawling institution that housed thousands of children, but its policies—such as the separation of children from their families—reflect the view of orphans as societal outcasts. Though the Foundling Hospital made significant strides in child care, its very existence as a monumental institution raised questions about the treatment of children in these systems.

5. **The Bethlehem Orphanage (Berlin, Germany):** "Founded" in the late 1800s, this orphanage was a vast, fortress-like structure located outside the city center of Berlin. Its size and architectural style were intended to evoke a sense of control and order. However, like many large orphanages of the time, it became a symbol of institutional neglect. The children housed here were

often subjected to long hours of work, minimal care, and poor living conditions. The institution's size and isolation added to the feeling of disempowerment that these children experienced.

Above: The ostentatious grandeur of the St. Joseph Orphanage, in Cleveland, Ohio, is pictured here in its former glory. Its lavish looks betray its sinister re-educational and indoctrinating purposes.

Go West, Young Man

The phrase *"Go West, young man"* is most often attributed to Horace Greeley, an American author and newspaper editor. He is believed to have popularized the phrase in an 1865 editorial in his newspaper, the *New York Tribune*.

However, the exact origin is a bit murky. While Greeley is widely credited, some evidence suggests the phrase may have originated earlier with John Babsone Lane Soule, who allegedly used it in an 1851 article in the *Terre Haute Express*.

Regardless of who first coined it, the phrase perfectly captured the spirit of westward expansion in the United States during the 19th century. It encouraged people to seek opportunity and a fresh start in the American West, which was depicted as a land of vast potential and untapped resources.

The *Orphan Trains* of the late 19th and early 20th centuries serve as a grim illustration of how orphaned and abandoned children were used to populate rural areas of the Midwest as well as a method of social control and indoctrination. Between 1854 and 1929, over 200,000 children were sent from orphanages in the eastern United States to the Midwest aboard "orphan trains," where they were placed with farming families in a bid to provide labor and foster a sense of moral duty. However, this practice also aligns with a broader agenda: by moving these children westward, away from the urban centers of influence, they were removed from environments where they could learn critical thinking and be exposed to diverse worldviews. Instead, these children were raised in rural settings, where they were more likely to be conditioned into conformity and compliance with the agricultural and Protestant work ethic that dominated the region. The Orphan Train Movement can thus be seen not only as an effort to repopulate the western territories but also as a deliberate attempt to create a more uniform, obedient population that would serve the goals of a greater societal transformation, laying the groundwork for a new world order based on conformity and compliance.

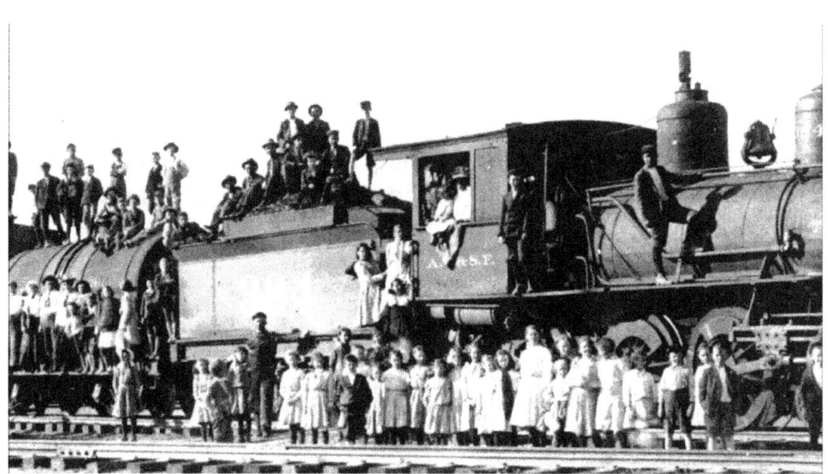

Pictured above: two distinct instances of orphan trains filled to the brim with the young.

Strange times. Some children were just too young to board the orphan train, and oddly enough, were sent by mail to go live with other family members cross-country.

The Establishment of a Board of Education

John D. Rockefeller's creation of the General Education Board (GEB) in 1902 was a deliberate step to centralize and control the American education system. The Board prioritized practical skills and vocational training to shape individuals into compliant workers for the industrial machine, aligning perfectly with the needs of burgeoning corporate interests. This system was not about fostering independent thought or creativity but about instilling discipline, punctuality, and conformity—qualities essential for an obedient workforce.

During the same period, orphanages were filled to capacity, many due to societal upheavals, poverty, and deliberate efforts to institutionalize those deemed unfit for society. These children, stripped of their families and heritage, became the raw material for an educational system designed to indoctrinate. The relocation of thousands of children via orphan trains served to break familial and cultural ties, making them more susceptible to the standardized narratives introduced by the GEB. These efforts worked hand in hand to erase memories of a divine past or Christ's millennial reign, replacing them with a secular, industrial vision of progress.

Rockefeller's education reforms were not merely coincidental developments but active measures to suppress critical thinking and reframe history to suit the needs of a burgeoning New World Order. By standardizing education and controlling the narratives taught to generations, the GEB laid the foundation for a society less likely to question authority or remember a spiritual legacy erased from mainstream history. This was indoctrination disguised as progress, aligning perfectly with the deception and control of Satan's Little Season.

John D. Rockefeller (1839-1937), U.S. businessman, investor and innovator? Or was he someone far more sinister?

Insane Asylums and the Erasure of Historical Memory

In the aftermath of Satan's release during his little season, a systematic reordering of society occurred, evident in the widespread institutionalization of individuals, particularly those who were perceived as a threat to the fabricated social order. The insane asylums of the late 19th and early 20th centuries acted as grim monuments to societal control, where millions of people, especially those who remembered or clung to the memories of the previous reign of Christ, were imprisoned. These asylums, often vast, imposing structures, housed thousands, and the criteria for being deemed "unfit" were astoundingly broad. It was shockingly easy to be declared insane during this period. A wide variety of causes were cited for commitment, including simple behaviors such as reading novels, being a woman in a challenging marriage, or suffering from "melancholy" after the death of a child.

In an era where dissent or deviation from the new norms was branded as madness, these institutions became a tool for silencing those who might still recall or practice the truths of the earlier millennial reign. Husbands could commit wives to asylums with little more than a claim of "hysteria" or "religious excitement," and many women were institutionalized for merely exhibiting strong opinions or defiance against patriarchal structures.

Such measures were not limited to women; the poor, the marginalized, and those exhibiting any form of dissent became targets. The authorities could arbitrarily decide that these individuals posed a risk to the new order and place them in asylums where they would be stripped of their dignity, their families, and their memory of a better time.

The grandiose architecture of the 19th and early 20th-century insane asylums, often marketed as symbols of hope and healing, defies rational explanation when scrutinized. These structures—some of the most lavish, intricate, and expensive buildings of their time—appear far too elaborate to serve the stated purpose of housing the mentally ill. Their sheer scale, complexity, and aesthetic grandeur suggest they were not built for their ostensible function but rather found—remnants of a previous advanced civilization, potentially from the era of Christ's millennial reign.

Take, for example, the Trans-Allegheny Lunatic Asylum, with its sprawling Gothic Revival design and capacity for thousands. Constructing such a monumental building with the rudimentary technology and limited resources of the 19th century strains credulity. Similarly, the Danvers State Hospital, with its turreted towers and intricate stonework, mirrors the architectural majesty of castles or cathedrals—structures that belonged to a far more sophisticated society than the one it was supposedly built for. These buildings were not constructed but rather found and re-purposed by the ruling elites, who rebranded them to fit their narrative of history while hiding the evidence of Christ's reign.

The theory gains even more traction when considering the overwhelming capacity of these asylums. Facilities such as Greystone Park Psychiatric Hospital, initially designed for 1,600 patients but cramming in over 7,000 at its peak, suggest a deliberate attempt to warehouse large swaths of the population. Were these individuals truly "mentally ill," or were they survivors of a cataclysmic reset—a remnant population that still remembered the divine rule of Christ and His resurrected saints? This reframing posits that those who clung to memories of the earlier civilization or resisted the imposed new order were labeled as insane and systematically confined.

Adding insult to injury, The Ruling Class's nefarious plan likely extended to isolating children from their families. This would explain the abundance of orphans during this period and the subsequent rise of orphan trains, which dispersed these children far and wide, erasing their ties to the truth. The grandeur of these asylums and their sinister role in the erasure of a godly past exposes them as tools of Satan's short season, used to cement control and perpetuate his version of history.

Notable examples of these asylums include:

1. **Trans-Allegheny Lunatic Asylum** (Weston State Hospital), West Virginia: This imposing Gothic Revival building could house over 2,400 patients at its peak.
2. **Danvers State Hospital**, Massachusetts: This asylum was housing up to 2,500 patients at its height.
3. **Eastern State Hospital**, Virginia: The first repurposed asylum in the U.S. (1770), though smaller compared to later ones, set the foundation for institutionalization.
4. **Greystone Park Psychiatric Hospital**, New Jersey: Eventually housing over 7,000 patients during its peak, it stood as one of the largest asylums in America.
5. **Hanwell Asylum, England**: One of the earliest and largest publicly funded asylums in the UK, housing thousands during the Victorian era.

Some of the characteristics of these asylums were the following:

Monumental Architecture Beyond Reason: The so-called 'insane asylums' of the 19th and early 20th centuries—such as the Trans-Allegheny Lunatic Asylum and the Danvers State Hospital—were far too grandiose to justify their stated purpose. These immense Gothic and Renaissance Revival-style complexes, boasting intricate stonework, soaring turrets, and expansive campuses, defy logic when paired with their alleged function as institutions for the mentally ill. Why would societies purportedly struggling with basic infrastructure and economy allocate resources to build structures rivaling royal palaces? The ruling elite's explanation falls apart under scrutiny, suggesting these buildings were not constructed but rather found—relics of a forgotten era, possibly the millennial reign of Christ.

Warehousing the 'Unfit': These vast institutions were designed to house thousands, with some far exceeding their original capacity. For instance, Greystone Park Psychiatric Hospital was initially designed for 1,600 but crammed in over 7,000. Were these individuals truly mentally ill, or were they survivors of a cataclysmic event—the release of Satan and the subsequent 'reset'? Survivors with memories of Christ's reign or dissenters refusing to conform to the new regime may have been deliberately labeled insane, imprisoned, and silenced. These asylums, then, became prisons for those who held onto inconvenient truths that contradicted The Ruling Class' fabricated narrative of history.

Erasing a Divine Past: The architectural sophistication of these asylums aligns not with the rudimentary technology of the 19th century but with the remnants of a superior civilization. Their apparent 'discovery' and re-purposing suggest an intentional cover-up by the ruling class during Satan's little season. By rebranding these buildings as asylums, The Ruling Class could systematically erase evidence of Christ's millennial reign, turning monuments of divine order into symbols of human despair.

The systematic institutionalization extended to children, with orphans being separated from families en masse and funneled into institutions or dispersed via orphan trains. This was no coincidence. Many of these children likely belonged to those confined in asylums, ensuring that any remaining connections to the earlier, godly civilization were severed. The massive orphanages of the time, like the imposing New York Foundling Hospital, echo the scale and nefarious intentions seen in the asylums.

Greystone Park Psychiatric Hospital in New Jersey is an architectural marvel. It was formerly known as: State Asylum for the Insane at Morristown.

An older picture of the Trans-Allegheny Lunatic Asylum feels ominous.

The Trans-Allegheny Lunatic Asylum still stands today, but merely as a
tourist attraction.

REASONS FOR ADMISSION
1864 TO 1889

INTEMPERANCE & BUSINESS TROUBLE	DISSOLUTE HABITS
KICKED IN THE HEAD BY A HORSE	DOMESTIC AFFLICTION
HEREDITARY PREDISPOSITION	DOMESTIC TROUBLE
ILL TREATMENT BY HUSBAND	DROPSY
IMAGINARY FEMALE TROUBLE	EGOTISM
HYSTERIA	EPILEPTIC FITS
IMMORAL LIFE	EXCESSIVE SEXUAL ABUSE
IMPRISONMENT	EXCITEMENT AS OFFICER
JEALOUSY AND RELIGION	EXPOSURE AND HEREDITARY
LAZINESS	EXPOSURE AND QUACKERY
MARRIAGE OF SON	EXPOSURE IN ARMY
MASTURBATION & SYPHILIS	FEVER AND JEALOUSY
MASTURBATION FOR 30 YEARS	FIGHTING FIRE
MEDICINE TO PREVENT CONCEPTION	SUPPRESSED MASTURBATION
MENSTRUAL DERANGED	SUPPRESSION OF MENSES
MENTAL EXCITEMENT	THE WAR
NOVEL READING	TIME OF LIFE
NYMPHOMANIA	UTERINE DERANGEMENT
OPIUM HABIT	VENEREAL EXCESSES
OVER ACTION OF THE MIND	VICIOUS VICES
OVER STUDY OF RELIGION	WOMEN TROUBLE
OVER TAXING MENTAL POWERS	SUPERSTITION
PARENTS WERE COUSINS	SHOOTING OF DAUGHTER
PERIODICAL FITS.	SMALL POX
TOBACCO & MASTURBATION	SNUFF EATING FOR 2 YEARS
POLITICAL EXCITEMENT	SPINAL IRRITATION
POLITICS	GATHERING IN THE HEAD
RELIGIOUS ENTHUSIASM	GREEDINESS
FEVER AND LOSS OF LAW SUIT	GRIEF
FITS AND DESERTION OF HUSBAND	GUNSHOT WOUND
ASTHMA	HARD STUDY
BAD COMPANY	RUMOR OF HUSBAND MURDER
BAD HABITS & POLITICAL EXCITEMENT	SALVATION ARMY
BAD WHISKEY	SCARLATINA
BLOODY FLUX	SEDUCTION & DISAPPOINTMENT
BRAIN FEVER	SELF ABUSE
BUSINESS NERVES	SEXUAL ABUSE & STIMULANTS
CARBONIC ACID GAS	SEXUAL DERANGEMENT
CONGESTION OF BRAIN	FALSE CONFINEMENT
DEATH OF SONS IN WAR	FEEBLENESS OF INTELLECT
DECOYED INTO THE ARMY	FELL FROM HORSE IN WAR
DERANGED MASTURBATION	FEMALE DISEASE
DESERTION BY HUSBAND	DISSIPATION OF NERVES

TRANS-ALLEGHENY LUNATIC ASYLUM

Above: The Trans-Allegheny Lunatic Asylum list of reasons to admit patients. Note the triviality and sheer madness (pun intended) of many of those. Of course, these would justify the thousands of people that were being forced into the then hell-hole.

Repopulating Under a New World Order

In the aftermath of significant global upheavals, such as wars and pandemics, there has often been a concerted effort to repopulate the world in line with new ideologies. During these periods, children—particularly those from displaced or marginalized communities—are often the most vulnerable. In *Satan's Little Season*, the notion of repopulating under a new world order goes beyond the survival of humanity, suggesting that the next generations are strategically raised and trained in a way that reinforces the power structures of the time. Whether through government-run institutions or religious movements, children become the blank slate upon which the future is written. The orchestration of family structures, societal norms, and even the cultural narratives surrounding identity and heritage is meticulously crafted to ensure that the next generation will grow up under the influence of an elite group who control the narrative of what the "new world" should look like. These efforts at repopulation are, therefore, not just about numbers but about the ideological transformation of society itself.

CHAPTER 9:

Further Theories and Speculations

"I was bold in the pursuit of knowledge, never fearing to follow truth and reason to whatever results they led, and bearding every authority which stood in their way."

~Thomas Jefferson

There are many questions that arise when exploring the possibility of the theories presented in this book. The pursuit of knowledge and truth presents multiple mental obstacles that can only be overcome by an increasingly open mind. Of course, I do not have all the answers—in fact, quite the opposite. I have, like you, perhaps, more questions than answers. And like you, I ask myself:

1. **If we are in the short season of Revelation 20:3, how long is a short season?**

2. **What does the idea of Christ's return already occurring mean for our view of salvation, the Kingdom of God, and the ultimate fulfillment of God's promises?**

3. Where is Christ now? And where are His saints who were said to rule for a thousand years? Are they back in heaven? At the North Pole? In another dimension? On another earth?

4. How do the events described in Revelation align with the historical timeline, and what role do the saints who reigned with Christ for a thousand years play in this?

5. How does the concept of a flat Earth, if taken literally, fit into this eschatological narrative?

6. If Jesus returned in the first century, how does this alter the course of history that we know today?

7. What historical evidence exists to suggest that key events, such as the reign of Christ, may have been intentionally obscured or reinterpreted over time?

8. Could there be more historical documentation that has been lost, hidden (perhaps in the Vatican's underground), or intentionally destroyed to prevent an accurate understanding of the timeline?

These are but a handful of the countless questions that weigh on my mind—and likely on yours as well. I cannot hope to answer them all within the pages of this book, or perhaps even in a lifetime, as I too am still searching.

That said, in this chapter, I will strive to explore some of these mysteries and, in doing so, perhaps uncover answers to a few of these persistent questions.

Melted Cities, Ruins, and Buildings

"The Lord is not slack concerning his promise, as some men count slackness; but is longsuffering to us-ward, not willing that any should perish, but that all should come to repentance. But the day of the Lord will come as a thief in the night; in the which the heavens shall pass away with a great noise, and the elements shall melt with fervent heat, the earth also and the

works that are therein shall be burned up. Seeing then that all these things shall be dissolved, what manner of persons ought ye to be in all holy conversation and godliness, looking for and hasting unto the coming of the day of God, wherein the heavens being on fire shall be dissolved, and the elements shall melt with fervent heat?" ~2 Peter 3:9-12

As we explore the shadowy remnants of once-thriving civilizations, we are confronted with strange and unsettling patterns—mysterious ruins, melted buildings, and cities that appear to have been scorched by an unseen force. These enigmatic remnants raise questions about what could have caused such widespread destruction, leaving these cities abandoned or reduced to rubble. The apostle Peter, in his second epistle, paints a vivid and catastrophic picture of the end of the age—a time when "the heavens shall pass away with a great noise, and the elements shall melt with fervent heat." This fiery dissolution speaks of an earth-shattering event, one that consumes not only the physical earth but the very creations of humankind.

While this imagery is often interpreted as a future event, it may be more accurately understood as referring to the judgment that occurred around 70-73 AD, or shortly thereafter, during the return of the Lord Jesus Christ as a Lion and as a King. The fall of Jerusalem, the destruction of the Temple, and the purging of the old covenant world align closely with the prophetic descriptions of fiery destruction in Scripture. This fiery judgment was not some distant future event, but rather a decisive moment in history that fulfilled the prophecies of the Old and New Testaments, signaling the end of one era and the establishment of another.

Evidence of such destruction can be found not only in biblical accounts but also in the physical ruins of ancient cities and civilizations scattered across the world. Among these, we find places like the Jiaohe Ruins in Turpan, Xinjiang, China. Once a bustling city along the Silk Road, Jiaohe now lies in desolation, its walls and structures showing signs of intense heat that appear to have melted or warped the very stone and mud bricks from which it was built. Archaeologists have long struggled to explain the source of this heat, which seems far beyond the typical fires or natural disasters known to have occurred in the region. Some scholars have even coined the term "meltology" to describe these ruins, where the effects of heat seem to have gone beyond what is traditionally expected.

Similarly, the ruins of Petra, the ancient city carved into the rock in modern-day Jordan, also present strange evidence of fire-like destruction. The city's structures, although primarily carved from rock, show signs of melting and heat exposure, with some surfaces appearing to have been altered by a force far beyond what natural processes alone could explain. The abandonment of Petra, like many ancient cities, could be seen as part of the divine judgment that took place at the time of Christ's return, which saw not only Jerusalem destroyed but also other prominent cities around the Roman Empire subjected to similar fiery fates.

These scattered ruins, marked by signs of intense heat and destructive forces, suggest that the imagery of the "elements melting with fervent heat" described the apostle Peter is not simply a metaphor for some far-off cosmic event but a description of the fiery judgment that befell the earth during or after the fall of Jerusalem and the destruction of the old covenant world. The elements of that world—its cities, its temples, its systems—were consumed in a divine conflagration that wiped away the old and made way for the new.

This view aligns with the eschatological perspective that sees Christ's return as a judgment that began in 70-73 AD, marking the end of the old era and the beginning of the establishment of the Kingdom of God under His rule. As such, the ruins we find around the world are not just remnants of ancient civilizations; they are also physical testaments to the judgment that was prophesied in the Bible and that came to pass with the return of Christ as the Lion of Judah and the King of Glory.

In this context, the strange ruins and melted cities found throughout the world make more sense. They can be seen as a confirmation of the prophetic declarations in Scripture. The destruction that Peter describes—the melting of the elements with fervent heat—was not just a spiritual event but a very physical one, one that affected the very fabric of the world's civilizations. It was, in a very real sense, Christ's great reset, just before His Millenium.

The mysterious Jiaohe Ruins of Turpan, Xinjiang, China, seem to be the remnants of buildings that melted through a strong heat.

Not all places are melted equal. Some show obvious signs of "meltology".

Above: Is this a strange rock formation, or ancient melted ruins?

The Mud Flood Hypothesis

The Mud Flood Hypothesis, when considered through the lens of Satan's Little Season, represents not just a physical catastrophe but a monumental reset of human civilization. This theorized event, occurring after Satan's release from the abyss (Revelation 20:7-8), aligns with the narrative of his efforts to deceive the nations and obliterate the evidence of Christ's millennial reign. The ramifications of the Mud Flood are vast, spanning physical destruction, societal upheaval, and the rewriting of history.

A Great Reset of Humanity

The Mud Flood acted as a literal and symbolic reset, erasing much of the progress and remnants of Christ's millennial kingdom. This event buried entire civilizations, advanced technologies, and architectural marvels, paving the way for Satan to institute a new order.

1. **Destruction of Millennial Evidence**: Structures such as star forts, cathedrals, and cities reflecting the glory of Christ's reign were submerged under layers of sediment, erasing their divine inspiration.
2. **Resetting Society**: By wiping out populations and severing cultural continuity, the Mud Flood allowed Satan and his followers to reshape the social and historical narrative in their favor.

Survivors and Their Fate

The survivors of this catastrophic reset faced three distinct paths, which mirror Satan's strategy of manipulation and control:

- **Recruitment**: Survivors were enlisted into Satan's ranks, possibly through coercion or deception, and became agents of his new world order.
- **Institutionalization**: Those who resisted or retained knowledge of the previous age were silenced, often placed in burgeoning insane asylums that doubled as prisons for inconvenient truths.
- **Orphaned Generations**: Children left behind were subjected to orphanages and programs such as orphan trains, where they were re-educated and disconnected from any knowledge of Christ's reign.

Evidence of a Reset

- **Architectural Anomalies**: The prevalence of buildings with buried floors and windows below street level suggests a layer of mud covering previously thriving civilizations.
- **Population Voids**: Historical accounts reveal sudden gaps in population numbers, indicating a mass die-off consistent with a global catastrophe.
- **Photographic Silence**: Early photographs of major cities depict empty streets and desolate infrastructure, suggesting a recent reset rather than long-standing urban development.

The Mud Flood also enabled Satan to rewrite history, introducing a false timeline and obscuring the divine truth. This reset aligns with the emergence of what theorists refer to as a phantom timeline, where fabricated events and figures replaced actual history. Educational and religious institutions, now under Satan's influence, propagated this revised narrative to ensure compliance and ignorance.

The World Fairs: A Veil for Historical Revisionism?

The World Fairs of the 19th and early 20th centuries stand as some of the most awe-inspiring events of modern history. Drawing millions of attendees from across the Earth, these fairs were ostensibly designed to showcase human ingenuity, industrial advancements, and artistic achievements. However, viewed through the lens of Satan's Little Season and the Great Reset, these fairs could be interpreted as deliberate efforts to reshape public perception, obscure the remnants of Christ's millennial reign, and present a false narrative of linear human progress.

Architectural Marvels and Mysterious Origins

At the heart of the World Fairs were their monumental structures, which, by official accounts, were often built in remarkably short timeframes using temporary materials such as wood and plaster. Yet, the sheer scale, intricate designs, and ornate details of these buildings have led many to question their origins:

- **The Chicago World's Fair (1893)**: The "White City" spanned over 600 acres, featuring grand neoclassical buildings, canals, and electric lighting—an unprecedented spectacle at the time. Critics argue that the supposed temporary structures displayed a level of craftsmanship inconsistent with their alleged impermanence.

- **The Paris Exposition Universelle (1889)**: Iconic structures like the Eiffel Tower were introduced, though some speculate that many other elaborate buildings on display were not newly constructed but remnants of an advanced past civilization repurposed for the fair.

- **The St. Louis World's Fair (1904)**: Known for its opulent pavilions, the fair purportedly showcased humanity's technological progress, yet many of the structures seemed to belong to an era far beyond the capabilities of their time.

If these structures were remnants of Christ's millennial reign, their destruction or disassembly post-fair could symbolize an intentional erasure of divine architecture, replacing it with the present narrative of human achievement.

World Fairs introduced the masses to technological marvels such as:

- **Electric Lighting and Moving Walkways**: Technologies that seemed to spring fully formed into existence, with little explanation of their development.

- **X-rays and Wireless Telegraphy**: While groundbreaking, the suddenness of these advancements raises questions about whether they were truly invented or merely rediscovered and presented as new.

- **Incubator Babies**: As seen earlier, one of the more startling exhibitions, premature babies cared for in incubators were displayed as curiosities, raising troubling ethical and spiritual questions.

Beyond the displays of technology, World Fairs served mostly as cultural and ideological showcases, subtly aligning attendees with the emerging narrative of the post-reset world:

- **Historical Revisionism**: Entire pavilions were dedicated to celebrating "progress," erasing or reframing older knowledge and civilizations.

- **Cultural Homogenization**: Indigenous and ancient cultures were often displayed as primitive or bygone, reinforcing the supremacy of modern industrial society.

- **Re-education and Influence**: With millions in attendance, these fairs became fertile grounds for spreading new ideologies, reinforcing state narratives, and conditioning the populace to accept the rewriting of their past.

World fairs and expositions have long been tools for shaping public perception and reframing the way populations view the world. Even as late as Montreal's Expo 1967, these events served as platforms for promoting specific narratives about the world we live in. Expo 1967, set during the Cold War era, emphasized themes of global unity and progress under the banner "Man and His World." It showcased space exploration (promoting NASA), communications, and modern architecture, subtly framing humanity's future as one of technological interdependence and global collaboration.

Through such exhibitions, world fairs didn't just display innovation; they actively shaped and reshaped cultural and social mindsets, constantly guiding and deceiving populations to embrace new ideologies about progress, globalism, and humanity's place in a rapidly evolving world.

Affluence Amid a Reset World

 The sheer opulence of the World Fairs—sprawling grounds, advanced infrastructure, and luxurious displays—contrasted starkly with the financial realities of the time, including global depressions and wars. If these events were orchestrated during Satan's Little Season, the resources and organization required for such spectacles might hint at the influence of powers seeking to dominate and manipulate a post-reset society.

Through this lens, the World Fairs appear not as celebrations of innovation but as tools for:

- **Erasing Evidence of Christ's Millennial Reign**: Presenting ancient or divine accomplishments as human achievements, effectively hiding the glory of the millennial kingdom.

- **Rewriting History**: Reinforcing the false timeline and suppressing the true chronology of humanity.

- **Normalizing State Control**: Through indoctrination and spectacle, preparing society to accept a new, satanically influenced order.

Once we scratch the surface and look into them, it is obvious that The World Fairs, which were hailed as triumphs of human ingenuity, served as a sophisticated mechanism to reshape history, hide divine truths, and further Satan's agenda during his Little Season. The architectural marvels, technological displays, and sheer scale of these events reveal a deeper, more insidious purpose—an intentional Great Reset, veiling the glorious past heritage of humanity and replacing it with a narrative of human-centered progress.

Looking west from Peristyle, Court of Honor and Grand Basin, Chicago World Fair, 1893

Crystal Palace, London World Fair, England,1934

Above: Vienna World's Fair, 1873

Pictured above: St Louis World's Fair, 1904.

The Suppressed Technologies of the Early 1900s

The early 1900s were a time of remarkable technological progress, with innovations that could have transformed society forever—yet many of these breakthroughs seem to have been intentionally suppressed or redirected by the ruling elite. Among these forgotten advancements were electric cars, airships (including dirigibles), rolling sidewalks, and other inventions that could have radically altered the trajectory of modern life. These technologies may have been remnants of the millennial age, a period of technological harmony and divine order, and the suppression of these innovations suggests a deliberate effort to replace them with systems that would benefit the ruling class and require the masses to pay exorbitant fees.

Electric cars, for example, were already in use and gaining traction in the early 20th century. Despite their practicality and efficiency, they were overshadowed by the rise of the internal combustion engine, largely driven by the oil industry. The global elite, including oil tycoons, deliberately worked to stifle electric vehicles, maintaining control over energy resources and ensuring ongoing profits from fossil fuels. Could this have been part of a broader, millennial-era energy system that was too decentralized and sustainable for the powers that be?

Airships and dirigibles were another exciting leap forward in transportation technology. With their elegant designs and ability to travel long distances without relying on the cumbersome infrastructure of railways or roads, airships like the Hindenburg offered the promise of global travel made accessible and affordable. However, after a series of high-profile accidents, the dirigible's promising future was abruptly cut short, and the development of this technology faded into obscurity. Airships had the potential to revolutionize transportation by providing large, fuel-efficient vessels capable of connecting distant parts of the world. Instead, The Ruling Class steered society toward the airplane industry, a far more expensive and resource-intensive form of air travel, ensuring that only the wealthy could afford to fly.

In addition to these advancements, inventions like rolling sidewalks, as seen in early 20th-century exhibitions and World's Fairs, hinted at a future of convenient, efficient urban living. These designs could have created smart cities with seamless public transportation, but instead, they were sidelined in favor of more expensive alternatives, such as cars, buses, and subways, which only served to line the pockets of powerful corporations. The technology for efficient mass transit was buried, ensuring that the people would remain dependent on The Ruling Class for their mobility.

These suppressed technologies may have been part of a broader, pre-established system that existed during Christ's millennial reign—a period of peace, prosperity, and technological harmony. The Ruling Class likely sought to erase any trace of these advancements, replacing them with systems that would perpetuate control and monopolize resources. By taking charge of the most promising technologies of the time, they maintained their financial dominance, trapping the masses in a cycle of dependence while burying a more sustainable, equitable way of life. The lost technologies of the early 1900s may represent the final remnants of a golden age— a time when the world was not ruled by profit and control, but by technological progress for the betterment of all.

Above: Thomas Edison poses with his first electric car, the Edison Baker, and one of its batteries. 1895.

Above: Air Ships, just one of the technologies that was eliminated from our past. Not only could they transport a lot more people than airplanes, but they were also much more cost efficient. Could this have led to their demise rather than the possibly staged Heidenburg explosion?

The North Pole: More than Just Ice and Snow?

One intriguing theory posits that Jesus Christ and the "camp of the saints" described in Revelation 20:9 are physically located at the North Pole. This idea arises from the biblical description of the camp being besieged by Satan and his forces upon his release. The remote and mysterious nature of the North Pole does align nicely with the idea of a hidden, protected sanctuary for Christ's millennial kingdom. Additionally, historical and mythological narratives often point to the North Pole as a mystical or sacred location.

Supporting Evidence for the Theory:

1. **Biblical Imagery of the North**: In Psalm 48:2, Mount Zion is described as being "on the sides of the north," symbolizing the city of the great King. This could metaphorically tie the North Pole to a divine or holy dwelling.

2. **Cartographic Mysteries**: Historical maps, such as the 16th-century Mercator maps, depict a magnetic mountain at the North Pole, surrounded by rivers and islands. These older maps often carry esoteric undertones, hinting at a hidden paradise that some link to the millennial reign.

3. **Aurora Borealis: A Reflection of God's Throne?** The awe-inspiring lights of the Aurora Borealis evoke a celestial beauty that some interpret as symbolic of God's divine throne. In Revelation 4:2-3, the throne of God is described as encircled by a rainbow resembling an emerald, with precious stones like jasper and carnelian illuminating the scene. Similarly, the vibrant and otherworldly colors of the northern lights—shimmering

greens, fiery reds, and ethereal purples—could be seen as a reflection of this biblical imagery.

The connection deepens when considering the heavenly city, the New Jerusalem, described in Revelation 21:18-21, where the city's foundation stones are adorned with every kind of jewel, radiating splendor and majesty. The interplay of light and color within the auroras mirrors this imagery, creating a visual metaphor for divine glory. These natural phenomena, often concentrated near the North Pole, could symbolize the sacredness of the region and its connection to a divine reality hidden from most of humanity.

Such interpretations suggest that the auroras may not merely be natural events but could instead serve as reminders or echoes of God's majesty, pointing to a greater significance tied to the mysteries of the millennial reign and Christ's throne.

4. **The Magnetic Pole: A Beacon**? The North Magnetic Pole has captivated humanity for centuries as a guiding force for navigation. Compasses, with their needles unwaveringly pointing north, emphasize the pole's central role as a natural lodestar. From a biblical or theological perspective, this magnetic phenomenon could be interpreted as a divine design, aligning with the concept of God as the ultimate guide and anchor for His creation.

The magnetic pole's unique properties reinforce the idea of the North Pole as a sacred and pivotal location. While the true North remains constant, the magnetic North shifts over time, moving unpredictably across the Earth's surface. This motion could be seen as symbolic.

Could the shifting magnetic pole point to something far greater than mere geography? Might it symbolize a divine direction, with its ever-changing position guiding humanity toward a heavenly destination? Could it be pointing to the Heavenly Jerusalem, the eternal dwelling of God and His saints? Or perhaps it is guiding us toward Christ the King Himself, whose reign is both eternal and unchanging, yet His influence and presence manifest in shifting ways on Earth?

The magnetic field, which both protects the earth and governs navigational systems, could further symbolize spiritual order and direction. In the context of millennial theories, this natural phenomenon underscores the potential for the North Pole to represent a profound spiritual and physical nexus—a place where heaven and earth converge in God's grand design

5. **Restricted Access**: The modern prohibition against exploring the polar regions, both North and South, freely raises questions about what might be concealed there. Some theorists argue this could be part of a larger effort to hide the truth about Christ's physical reign and presence on Earth—or even to hide other lands. But that is for another book altogether.

The 1595 Mercator Map of the North Pole Regions (above) offers much food for conjecture. Pictured below is a close-up of what is found at its center: The Rupes Nigra, or Black Rock.

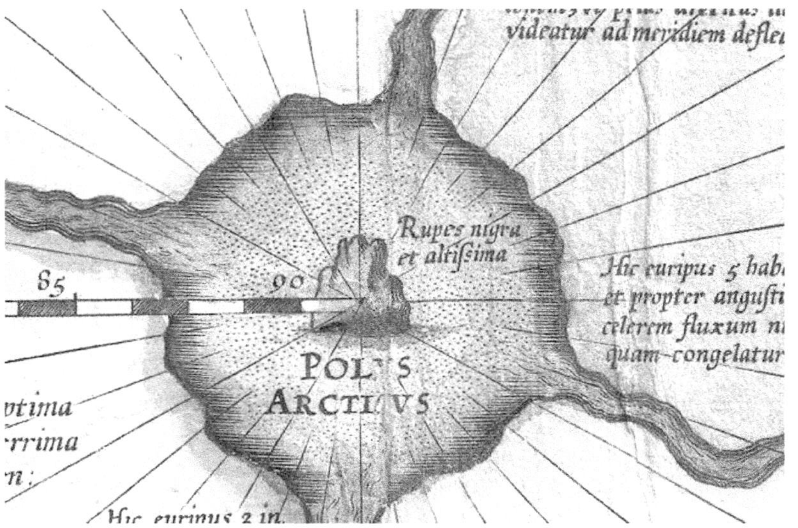

A close-up of Mercator's map shows the *Rupes Nigra,* or *Black Stone,* surrounded by a giant whirlpool, four rivers, and four continents. In the book "The Smoky God", these four rivers are said to bear the same names as the rivers in Eden: Pishon, Gihon, Hiddekel, and Euphrates. Some have surmised this "Black Stone" at The North Pole could be none other than Mount Zion, the mountain where God is said to reside, spoken of abundantly in Scripture. Also worth noting is the striking pattern formed by the four masses of land and the four rivers in Eden—it closely resembles a swastika. In ancient times, this symbol held positive or neutral meanings, far removed from the negative connotations it carries in modern times.

Today, however, the name "Blackstone" has been adopted by an The Ruling Class investment firm, which ironically manages the world's largest alternative assets—$1 trillion in total. As we trace the flow of money, intriguing clues begin to emerge. In the Satan's world of power and influence, there are no coincidences.

Where Are Jesus and the Saints Right Now?

The question of where Jesus the Millennial saints currently reside is both intriguing and profound, offering a glimpse into the mysteries of eschatology and the heavenly realm. Based on Scripture and theological speculation, here is an exploration of their possible locations.

Revelation 20:9 refers to "the camp of the saints," which some interpret as a physical place on earth. I believe this camp is located at or near the North Pole, possibly even within (as "in" or "under") the earth, in an area shielded from the prying eyes of humanity. This secluded and protected dwelling could serve as a base for the resurrected saints—those who reigned with Christ during the Millennial Kingdom.

These saints, who now exist in glorified, resurrected bodies, may still intervene in the affairs of earth from this hidden location. Who knows? It is conceivable that their activities remain unseen to us during Satan's little season, aligning with the theme of God's kingdom being both present yet concealed in its fullness. Some have suggested that this "camp" might even be a gateway to greater spiritual realms, offering the saints direct access to Christ.

As for Jesus Christ, I believe He currently resides in the New Jerusalem—the glorious, heavenly city described in Revelation 21. This city is unlike anything humanity has ever known, with its dimensions revealing a perfect cube: 12,000 stadia by 12,000 stadia by 12,000 stadia, or roughly 1,500 miles on each side. Its walls, measuring 144 cubits high (approximately 200 feet), speak to its magnificence and impenetrability.

This city-state is not merely a symbolic representation but a literal, physical place where the glory of God dwells. However,

I believe it is currently cloaked, hidden from human sight and undetected by our technologies. The New Jerusalem exists as a spiritual and physical reality, awaiting its ultimate unveiling at the culmination of God's plan.

While I believe Jesus resides in the New Jerusalem, I do not believe He is detached from His saints or the earth. Mount Zion, of Rupes Nigra—as we have seen earlier, often symbolized as a spiritual and physical connection between heaven and earth, could serve as a means by which the saints in their resurrected bodies have access to the Lord. It is also likely that Christ, in His glorified state, visits the camp of the saints regularly, maintaining a direct relationship with His faithful ones who rule under His authority.

This dual dynamic—Jesus in the New Jerusalem and the saints on earth—represents the continuation of God's kingdom work during Satan's little season. The saints serve as His representatives on earth, still guiding humanity, albeit in a limited way, while Christ reigns supreme from His heavenly throne, preparing for the final fulfillment of God's eternal plan.

The notion of a cloaked New Jerusalem and a hidden camp of the saints aligns, I believe, with the theme of God's kingdom being veiled to those outside of faith. As Jesus Himself said, "The kingdom of God does not come with observation; nor will they say, 'See here!' or 'See there!' For indeed, the kingdom of God is within you" (Luke 17:20-21). While this may speak of the spiritual nature of the kingdom, it also leaves room for the possibility of a concealed, literal manifestation of His rule.

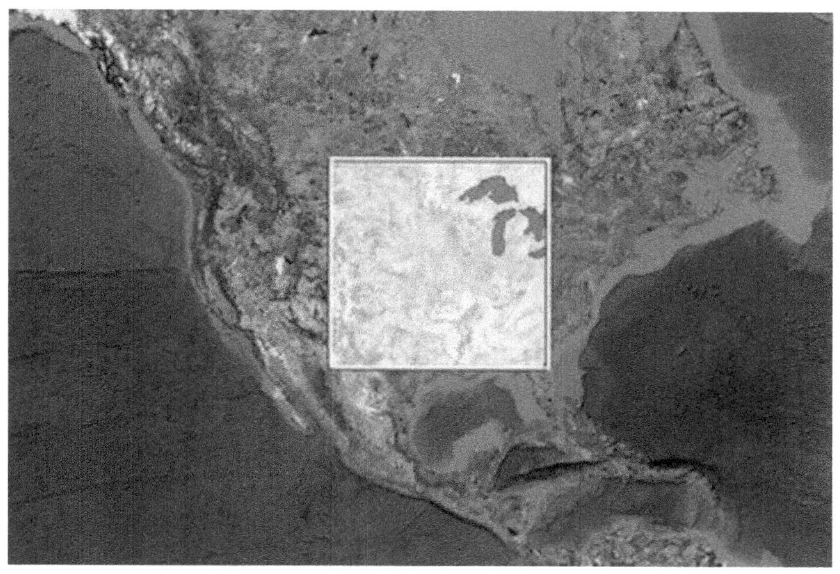

This image shows the approximate dimensions of the New Jerusalem.
It is a massive City-State whence the Lord reigns.

CHAPTER 10:

A Chronology of Little Season Deceptions

"There are two ways to be fooled. One is to believe what isn't true; the other is to refuse to believe what is true."
~Soren Kierkegaard

During the millennium of Christ, Satan was bound, confined to the abyss, and unable to exert his influence over the nations and humanity. This forced hiatus provided a unique opportunity for him to reflect deeply and strategize, a thousand years during which the adversary was free from the chaos he typically sowed. In the silence of his confinement, one can only imagine Satan pondering his past failures and contemplating how to manipulate the hearts of humanity upon his eventual release. He would have meticulously analyzed the patterns of human behavior, the vulnerabilities of nations, and the weaknesses of individuals. This time of introspection was no doubt used by the Enemy as a strategic withdrawal, allowing him to prepare for the moment he would re-emerge into a world renewed, yet still very susceptible to deception.

Upon his release, Satan was poised to unleash his carefully crafted arsenal of strategies designed to gradually seduce the nations. With a unique understanding of the human psyche and motivations, he sought to exploit the very weaknesses he had observed for millennia prior. Armed with the pondered insights and a battle plan gained over a millennium, he launched a multi-faceted approach, employing manipulation, division, and the seduction of power to lead people, the Church, and nations astray.

The following dates and events are, of course, theoretical approximations based on a synthesis of historical patterns, biblical interpretations, and speculative research. While they provide a framework for understanding how Satan's Little Season may have unfolded, the precise timing and details remain conjecture at best. The goal is not to present an exact chronology, but to highlight key themes and strategies that align with Scripture and historical anomalies. As you read and ponder, I encourage you to discern the broader picture of deception and its impact on our present world.

1. The End of the Millennium and Satan's Release (Approx Late 1600s - Early 1700s)

- **The Saints Depart:** At the close of Christ's Millennial reign, the Saints vacate the Millennial cities, possibly to the North Pole, or to an undisclosed location (Isaiah 26:20). This absence leaves the world vulnerable to Satan's schemes.

- **Satan Loosed from the Pit:** Revelation 20:7 marks the unleashing of Satan, igniting a period of global deception.

2. The Mudflood Catastrophe and Global Reset (1700s)

- **The Mudflood Events:** A (possible) catastrophic global deluge of mud buries ancient cities and civilizations, leaving countless dead and survivors dazed, confused, and disoriented.

- **Elite Bargain with Satan:** Having bid their time for generations while he was in the pit, powerful families (Satan's seedline) make a pact with Satan (their father) for dominion, wealth, and influence over the remnants of humanity.

3. The Abandoned Cities and Rise of Freemasonry (1700s - 1800s)

- **Reclaiming Ancient Cities:** The Ruling Class take control of vacated millennial cities, rebranding themselves as "founders", "builders", and "establishers" (e.g., Freemasonry).

- **Repurposing Millennial Structures:** Churches, orphanages, insane asylums, and World's Fair structures are retrofitted to align with the new narrative.

- **Luciferian Foundations:** Secret societies like the Freemasons emerge as tools for rewriting history and spreading Satanic influence.

4. The Rewriting of History and the Indoctrination of the Masses (1800s)

- **Historical Revisionism:** Satan's agents erase and distort records of the Millennial Kingdom, crafting a secular, godless timeline to replace divine history.

- **Orphan Trains and Repopulation:** Children are relocated to repopulate cities under new rulers, ensuring their indoctrination into the false narrative.

- **Silencing Dissent:** Insane asylums and prisons are used to confine those who remember the truth or resist the new order.

5. Scientific and Cultural Subversion (1800s - Early 1900s)

- **Invention of Evolution:** Darwin's theories replace biblical creation with naturalistic explanations, undermining faith in God. Other philosophers of the enlightenment era also are pushed to the forefront of Academia to gradually overtake Christian thought.

- **Technological Suppression:** Advancements like free energy, airships, and electric cars are sabotaged to maintain elite control over resources.

- **World's Fairs:** These events serve as cover-ups for the destruction of millennial artifacts and an opportunity to showcase the new narrative of "The New World Order" and indoctrinate the masses.

6. Wars and Economic Manipulation (1900s)

- **Global Wars:** Elite families orchestrate conflicts (e.g., World Wars) to consolidate power, further destroy evidence of the past, and reset societal structures.

- **Central Banking:** Institutions like the Federal Reserve create economic systems designed to enslave humanity through debt and fiat currencies.

- **Mass Media Propaganda:** Control of mass media ensures the dominance of Satanic ideologies and distracts humanity from spiritual truths.

7. Apostasy and Spiritual Deception (1900s - Present)

- **Infiltration of Religion:** Seminaries and church hierarchies are subverted, leading to a reformatting of theology, ecumenism, and apostate movements.

- **Rise of New Age and Secularism:** Spiritual deception flourishes through humanism, secularism, churchianity, and false eschatologies.

8. Technological Control and Globalization (2000s - Present)

- **Surveillance/Police State:** Advances in technology are weaponized for mass surveillance, ensuring total control over populations.

- **Transhumanism and AI:** Humanity is lured into a Satanic vision of "evolution" through artificial intelligence, genetic manipulation, mass immunization programs, genetically modified organisms (GMOs), and the introduction of fluoridated water, subtly altering the human body and mind to align with an anti-God agenda.

- **Pandemics and Fear Tactics:** Manufactured crises are used to tighten elite control and condition society for the final global order.

9. The Final Push Toward the New World Order (2000s - Present)

- **Global Secularism:** A universal belief system rooted in humanism, moral relativism and faith in "the universe," stripped of Christ's truth and authentic Christianity, paves the way for widespread deception.

- **Censorship and Persecution:** True biblical Christianity is further targeted as extremist, paving the way for an eventual total censorship of biblical truth.

- **The Last Great Deception:** Satan's final schemes culminate in a global system that defies God, setting the stage for the ultimate judgment.

10. Satan's Last-Ditch Effort to Wage War Against God (Future Event)

- **The Final Deception:** Satan launches one last, desperate attempt to deceive the nations, rallying them from the four corners of the earth—Gog and Magog—for a climactic battle.

- **The Gathering of the Nations:** With numbers as vast as the sand of the sea, these deceived forces encircle the camp of the saints and the beloved city, intent on destroying God's people and challenging His rule.

- **Divine Intervention:** In a definitive act of judgment, fire from heaven consumes the gathered armies, signifying the futility of Satan's rebellion.

- **Eternal Defeat:** The devil is (finally) cast into the lake of fire and brimstone, where he joins the beast and the false prophet, enduring eternal torment as justice is fully realized.

The Gog and Magog War

In his final act of deception, could Satan manipulate humanity into believing that the saints and the beloved city represent a threat to the world? The passage in Revelation 20:7–10 describes the nations rallying against the camp of the saints, an even known in eschatology as the Gog and Magor war. But the mechanism of such a colossal mobilization remains unexplained. A plausible conjecture is that Satan might exploit humanity's growing fascination with extraterrestrial life and advanced technology, along with the government's current willingness to disclose information about UFOs, to weave a grand deception.

Imagine a scenario where the saints, protected and gathered in a divine location, are portrayed by Satan as hostile extraterrestrials or an existential threat to Earth's survival. Using advanced propaganda, artificial intelligence, and the control of global media, Satan could frame their divine presence as an alien invasion or a danger to human progress.

By appealing to fear and the promise of global unity against a "common enemy," Satan could galvanize the nations into a final war.

This deception would align with humanity's increasing detachment from spiritual truth, as many have already embraced materialistic and naturalistic worldviews. Satan, the master of lies, could exploit this mindset to turn humanity's fear of the unknown into a rallying cry for war. The armies, unknowingly fighting against God's chosen people, would fulfill the prophecy in Revelation, their rebellion culminating in divine judgment.

This potential scenario aligns disturbingly well with former President Ronald Reagan's famous speech, where he mused about the unifying effect of an alien threat. Reagan suggested that a common enemy from beyond our planet could dissolve human divisions, forging global unity. In this prophetic context, the introduction of false extraterrestrial entities could exploit this concept, rallying the nations under a single banner and fostering a deceptive sense of shared purpose and righteousness. Echoing President Reagan's thoughts, are those of Wernher von Braun, who was a German-American aerospace engineer and space architect. He was a member of the Nazi Party and Allgemeine SS, the leading figure in the development of rocket technology in Nazi Germany, and later a pioneer of rocket and space technology in the United States. Just before he died in 1977, he told his secretary, Carol: *"And remember Carol, the last card is the alien card. We are going to have to build space-based weapons against aliens and all of it is a lie."*

So, as the masses fixate on this fabricated alien menace, they would unwittingly align with Satan's deceptive agenda, turning their focus away from the spiritual conflict at hand. This grand illusion would serve multiple purposes: distracting nations from the truth of Christ, consolidating power under a single global authority, and ultimately targeting the saints, who remain steadfast in the camp of righteousness.

The drone sightings of late December 2024 could be interpreted as an initial test—a controlled introduction to the idea that humanity faces threats from the skies. These sightings spark curiosity and unease, laying the psychological groundwork for a larger, more intricate deception involving false extraterrestrial beings. Such entities, posing as superior and benevolent or even threatening alien forces, would manipulate global perceptions. Nations might be convinced they are engaged in a war against a cosmic adversary, while the true target of their aggression—the camp of the saints—is cast as the focal point of this conflict.

As nations rally against this fabricated threat, they unwittingly align themselves with the forces of darkness, their consciousness reshaped to embrace a false worldview. This ultimate deception is designed not only to target the saints but also to blind the world to the reality of Christ's reign and the impending judgment.

In this way, the final great deception would serve as the culmination of all previous strategies, uniting the world under a shared delusion and propelling humanity toward its final confrontation with the truth—Christ and His righteous ones.

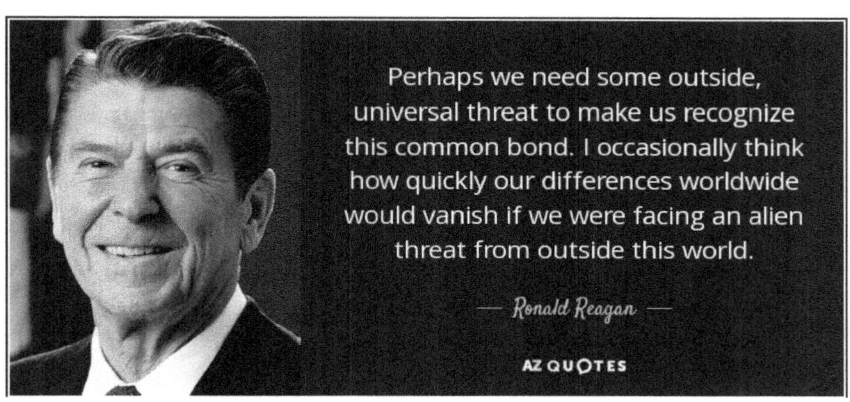

Above: Was U.S. President Ronald Reagan merely conjecturing? Was he prophesying? Did he know some secret future plans by the governments of the world?

CONCLUSION

Shortly after his re-election in November 2024, U.S. President Donald Trump mentioned in a speech that he wanted to bring back World Fairs. He noted that this would be similar to The New York World Fair of 1939, the Chicago World Fair of 1893, and The Nashville World Fair of 1897. President-Elect Trump also alluded to claims of 'free energy' technology utilizing Tesla towers and Aether during those fairs.

Ex Canadian Premier Justin Trudeau, in his speech at the U.N. during the 2020 pandemic, stated, *"This pandemic has provided an opportunity for a reset."* It becomes clear that the "reset" spoken of may not be one of renewal or moral restoration, but rather a recalibration of the world's power structures—an agenda that aligns with the rise of a global elite, whose vision is not for the betterment of mankind, but for its subjugation.

Knowing what we know now about the "resets" and the hidden purposes and true nature of the World Fairs, this development presages nothing good. These expos were not merely about showcasing advancements in technology and culture, they were vehicles for ushering in control mechanisms, and influencing public perception on a massive scale. The connection to "free energy" technologies, which many believe were suppressed for economic or geopolitical reasons, is particularly concerning. It could signify a return to a communist-style system that seeks to centralize power, restrict true progress, and monopolize innovation for those in control—perhaps a key part of the broader agenda to control humanity's future.

What we are witnessing is part of a larger, more sinister pattern that fits into the prophetic narrative of Satan's "little season" described in Revelation 20:3. The world is being primed for a time of unparalleled deception, where the boundaries between truth and falsehood become blurred further, and where the masses will willingly follow a false vision of progress, security, and prosperity. This season will be marked by the further infiltration of lies into every aspect of life, reshaping society under the guise of advancement and benevolence.

As we face this coming period, it's crucial for believers and truth-seekers to stay vigilant and discerning. The seduction of the nations will not come with warning signs or clear markers; instead, it will be wrapped in the allure of new technologies, a promise of peace and government protection, and a seductive vision of a "better" future. But beneath it all, there will be a lie—the same lie that Satan has used from the beginning, that we can build a utopia without God, relying instead on our own understanding and power.

A Not-So-Bright Future

Under the rapid march of technological and societal advancements they promise progress, but lurking beneath the surface is a darker reality. As humanity ventures into uncharted territory, the potential for control, manipulation, and loss of freedom looms ever larger. What is introduced as innovation may, in fact, be paving the way for a dystopian future where human autonomy and authenticity are sacrificed on the altar of convenience and power. The main culprits to watch out for are:

1. Artificial Intelligence and Automation

- **AI dominance:** Societies increasingly surrender decision-making to AI, risking a future where human autonomy is sidelined by algorithmic control.
- **Job elimination:** Automation threatens to displace millions, creating widespread unemployment and dependence on more government systems.
- **Human-machine fusion:** Brain-computer interfaces blur the line between man and machine, leading to a further loss of individuality and free will.

2. The Metaverse and Digital Realities

- **Escaping reality:** Entire populations will retreat into artificial worlds, abandoning the challenges of real life and allowing societal decay.
- **Digital slavery:** The metaverse will become a tool for total surveillance and control, locking individuals into an inescapable virtual panopticon.
- **Economic entrapment:** Virtual economies controlled by corporations will deepen wealth gaps and strip users of ownership.

3. Genetic Engineering and Biohacking

- **Designer humanity:** Editing DNA through vaccines, drugs, and GMOs to "improve" humans, risks creating genetic castes and exacerbating social inequality.
- **Unintended consequences:** Genetic modifications could unleash unforeseen (or planned) diseases and/or destabilize ecosystems.
- **Surveillance health:** Implantable devices are said to offer health insights but also grant governments or corporations very invasive access to personal data.

4. Energy Innovations

- **Fusion monopoly:** Fusion energy will become a weapon of control, exploited by the few at the expense of the many.
- **Wireless power risks:** Power transmitted invisibly has many negative effects on personal health and populations.
- **False sustainability:** Most new "green" technology masks resource exploitation and a hunger for profits, and seeks to hide environmental destruction under a veneer of progress.

5. Global Governance and Socioeconomic Shifts

- **Digital currency enslavement:** Centralized digital currencies could give governments unprecedented power to track, restrict, or even freeze individual transactions.
- **UBI dependency:** Universal Basic Income (UBI), when rolled out, will create a society wholly dependent on the state, annihilating initiative and freedom.
- **Global technocracy:** Centralized power in transnational bodies will erode national sovereignty and enforce a homogenized satanic global agenda.

6. Climate Engineering and Sustainability

- **Geoengineering dangers:** Manipulation and weaponization of the weather will surely backfire, leading to many more unintended natural disasters as well as fabricated ones.
- **Synthetic food control:** Vertical farming and artificial food production may lead to a centralized

control of food supplies, making populations vulnerable to the worse kind of manipulation.

- **Eco-fascism:** Under the guise of sustainability, personal freedoms and property rights will be stripped away further.

7. Post-humanism and Transcendence

- **Loss of humanity:** Integrating technology into the human body will lead to the erosion of what makes us uniquely human and, in the process, destroy what makes us "into the image of God".
- **Machine overlords:** Artificial consciousness will undoubtedly surpass human intellect, posing existential risks when it becomes uncontrollable.
- **Digital immortality deception:** Promises of eternal life through consciousness uploading, a plan well under way by Big Tech, will trap souls in artificial systems, severing their connection to God, and potentially ruining their chance for salvation.

As we march further along into Satan's little season, each of these developments carries clear ominous potential. In the name of scientism, innovation and progress, humanity is trading even more freedom and authenticity for more government control and illusion. Smart cities are at the forefront of this ominous shift, often presented as the pinnacle of technological progress. Under the guise of efficiency, sustainability, and connectivity, these urban centers are bound to become surveillance hubs, tracking every movement, transaction, and interaction of their inhabitants—the ideal prisons without bars. While marketed as a utopian ideal, smart cities are poised to become digital prisons, where privacy is sacrificed and citizens are managed like data points in a grand system of control. Far from fostering true freedom, they will serve as the blueprint for a future where autonomy is a relic of the past.

So, for those with eyes to see and ears to hear, the signs are clear. It is time to awaken to the reality of this "little season" and prepare ourselves mentally, physically, and spiritually for dire times ahead.

Keep Seeking Truth, No Matter What

My awakening to the many novel theological and eschatological ideas presented in this book was both challenging and transformative. I'll be honest, though. At first, I was negatively affected, even depressed. I felt a deep sense of loss; of mourning, as though I had arrived too late to witness the most magnificent event in human history: the Marriage Supper of the Lamb and the glorious thousand-year reign of Christ and His saints on Earth. I always thought I'd be a part of that. So, for me, it was as if the celebration had passed, leaving only faint echoes of its splendor in the pages of scripture and history.

But alongside this initial disappointment came an even greater gift: gratitude. I found myself profoundly thankful to realize that my Lord and Savior, Jesus Christ, had been faithful to every promise He made. He had indeed returned, just as He said He would, and His kingdom had come in its perfect time and season. This realization brought me not only comfort, but also a renewed sense of purpose—even joy.

Make no mistake, the unveiling of these truths—no matter how disorienting at first—is a blessing. Each revelation I encountered lifted yet another veil, allowing me to see more clearly the timeline of God's work in human history and the season we find ourselves in now. Truth has a way of shaking our foundations, but it also builds new ones, stronger and more aligned with God's purposes.

If you, too, feel shaken or even disheartened by these new revelations, take heart. The pursuit of truth is never in vain. Jesus Himself declared that knowing the truth would set us free (John 8:32). The journey may be unsettling, but it is through discomfort that we grow, through questioning that we find answers, and through seeking that we truly come to know Him.

Remember, the Kingdom of God is not only in what was but in what is and is to come. Even now, His Spirit is still at work, calling and empowering us, His people, to live boldly, love deeply, and shine as lights in a world ever so clouded by deception.

So, be encouraged. Though the path of truth may be narrow and challenging, it leads to life and freedom. The fact that you are seeking it—willing to question, learn, unlearn, and grow—means that God is already at work in your heart and mind. So, no matter how you may be feeling as you reach the end of this book, this is not the end of your journey. Rather, it is a powerful new beginning. Trust the Father to guide you, and let His truth shape your understanding and deepen your faith.

In the meantime, may we look forward to His making All things right, and to New Heavens and a New Earth. Being in Christ provides the hope of victory and eternal life—no matter what. God's tabernacle will be with us, and we shall be His people forever and ever. Amen.

Revelation 21:3-5:

"And I heard a great voice out of heaven saying, Behold, the tabernacle of God is with men, and he will dwell with them, and they shall be his people, and God himself shall be with

them, and be their God. And God shall wipe away all tears from their eyes; and there shall be no more death, neither sorrow, nor crying, neither shall there be any more pain: for the former things are passed away. And he that sat upon the throne said, Behold, I make all things new. And he said unto me, Write: for these words are true and faithful."

About the Author

Theo Rhising lives with his wife and three children. A man of deep faith, he has spent over two decades exploring the hidden intersections of biblical prophecy, historical enigmas, and conspiratorial agendas. Passionate about uncovering the truth behind history, spiritual mysteries and societal deceptions, Rhising tackles topics that many shy away from, shedding light on the dark corners of history and theology.

His fascination with ancient texts, ancient enigmatic ruins, conspiracies, secret societies, and even cryptids adds a unique layer to his writing, blending both faith and the unexplained. Whether unraveling eschatological puzzles or examining the evidence of Satan's influence in the modern world, Rhising's work dares readers to question everything they've been taught and invites them to seek answers rooted in scripture and critical inquiry. It's no coincidence that his chosen pen name, Theo Rhising (theorizing), reflects his passion for exploring, questioning, and speculating about theological truths—what else could you expect from someone so aptly named?

Through his writing, he challenges readers to think deeply, confront unsettling possibilities, and broaden their understanding of the times we live in. Living in the quiet of rural Eastern Canada, Rhising balances his investigative pursuits with his role as a devoted husband and father, continuously inspired by God, creation, reality, and the mysteries that surround us.

Also from Wild Remnant Publishing:

The North Pole and Inner Earth Chronicles

Explore the Uncharted Depths of Earth's Mysteries in this Landmark Two-Book Compilation of The Smoky God and The Secret Diary of Admiral Richard E. Byrd

Uncover the secrets of the uncharted and delve into the enigmatic realms of inner Earth, beyond the North Pole, with this captivating compilation of two classic works about the hollow or inner Earth: ***The Smoky God: A Voyage to the Inner World*** by *Willis George Emerson* and ***The Secret Diary of Admiral Richard E. Byrd.***

The Smoky God: A Voyage to the Inner World takes you on a remarkable journey. Follow the adventures of Olaf Jansen as he recounts a mysterious voyage into the heart of our realm, through the North Pole, as recorded from his deathbed confession. Navigating the uncharted polar regions with his father, Jansen discovers a hidden civilization of giants and its awe-inspiring landscapes, captivating readers with vivid descriptions of an underground utopia.

The Secret Diary of Admiral Richard E. Byrd. This intriguing document chronicles Admiral Richard Evelyn Byrd's purported exploration of the Arctic's mysterious interior. Within its pages lies an account of a journey that challenges conventional beliefs about the shape of our Earth, provoking the imagination with its amazing tales of a hidden and highly advanced civilization residing past the boundaries of polar ice caps.

The North Pole and Inner Earth Chronicles © invites readers to indulge in these timeless explorations, sparking curiosity about the unknown and challenging established beliefs about our world. It is perfect for conspiracy researchers, adventurers, mystery enthusiasts, and for all those with a thirst for exploration and discovery.

This landmark edition also features:

- **Unabridged original accounts**
- **Pictures and maps**
- **A foreword by Sebastien Richard**

The Smoky God: A Voyage to the Inner World and **The Secret Diary of Admiral Richard E. Byrd** merge in this unique compilation to offer readers a captivating narrative that has fascinated generations.

Delight your mind's eye as you delve into these fascinating expeditions and accounts of the unknown depths of our earth realm.

Ancient Cryptids Anthology:

A Rare Collection of Classic Writings and Historical Accounts on Dogman, Bigfoot, Wendigo

Explore the primal fear of cryptids through the eyes and beliefs of ancient American and European cultures.

Delve into *Ancient Cryptids Anthology* ©, where you'll encounter historical writings and accounts about three enigmatic creatures: Bigfoot, Dogman, and the Wendigo. This voluminous compilation features three classic full-length books-in-one:

- ***The Book of Werewolves*** by Sabine Baring-Gould (1865)
- ***The Bauman Story*** by Theodore Roosevelt (1893)
- ***The Wendigo*** by Algernon Blackwood (1910)

Beyond these foundational texts, you'll also find:

- **An Introduction by Bestselling Author Kyle Steel** who offers keen insights and sets the tone for exploring ancient cryptid legends.

- **Illustrations and Historical Pictures** which enhance your reading experience.

- **Ancient Cryptid Case Files** that present compelling, real-world accounts documenting cryptid encounters through the ages.

- **A Readable, User-Friendly Format** with an easy-to-read 12 pt font for comfort and accessibility.

This enthralling anthology provides many gripping tales like *The 1924 Bigfoot abduction of Albert Ostman, The Beast of Gévaudan, The Swift Runner Wendigo Case,* and many more, which blend chilling folklore with firsthand historical accounts. It boldly takes readers deep into the foreboding wildernesses of ancient North America and Europe, where encounters with cryptids like Bigfoot, Dogman, and Wendigo blurred the line between myth and living horror.

Perfect for both seasoned cryptid enthusiasts and curious newcomers, this unique book chronicles centuries-old reports and provides a fascinating glimpse into historical encounters with these notorious creatures. As modern interest in these mysterious beings continues to surge, these legendary stories ignite fascination about our shared connection to the unknown, our collective past, and our very uncertain future.

ENJOYED THIS BOOK?

If so, please be kind and leave a review on: